COMPUTER NETWORKING COURSE

Learn the basic tools of the computer networking from the bottom up in 20 minutes a day. Planning the networks and configuring the windows servers

Table of Contents

Introduction 1

Chapter 1: Computer Networking.............................3

  Types of System... 4

  Wireless Networks...10

  System Models 11

  The Internet Framework 17

  Addresses and Numbers...................................... 32

Chapter 2: Storage Architecture 51

  Network Attached Storage (NAS) 52

  Execution versus limit....................................... 59

  The I/O data Patterns.. 60

  Structuring the capacity framework 63

  Virtualization Architecture............................... 66

Chapter 3: Transmission control protocol (TCP) and IMPLEMENTATION...75

  Overview of TCP..75

  Round Trip Time (RTT) 85

Chapter 4: Planning a Network 90

  Organization set up 90

  Strategy and Culture.. 92

  Options Analysis 98

  System Design Tools and Algorithms 105

  Network Topology 107

Chapter 5: WIDE AREA NETWORK....................115

  Point to Point services 119

Chapter 6: Configuration 129

Windows servers 129

  Essential steps of configuring a new server 134

Conclusion 147

Description 149

Introduction

In this book *Computer networking* course, you will *learn the basic tools of computer networking from the bottom up. You will learn about planning the networks and configuring the windows servers.*

The chapters will cover a wide range of subtopics that will leave you enlightened and knowledgeable about basic computer networking skills. Chapter one of the book gives you an insight into networking. Here, you will learn on the types of systems, and also get to understand more on the wireless networks. Further, this chapter takes you into details of the Internet. Here, the book dives into the history of the internet, and also the pros and cons of the internet. You will also get to learn about Addresses and numbers.

Chapter two of the book covers the storage architecture. Here, you will learn the various storage mechanisms in networking. You may be using the storage systems but do not know how the systems work. Well, you will learn it here in the simplest form possible. This includes the network-attached storage, storage area network, tape and tape libraries. Structuring the capacity framework is also discussed into details as well as virtualization architecture. The third chapter discusses transmission control protocol and implementation the book will strategically explain to you what this means. You will learn the layers of TCP as well as the benefits and downfalls. The book will introduce and give you the details of Round trip time.

The fourth chapter of the book discusses the planning of a network. The author dives into the organization set up, strategy and culture and also options analysis. Through this chapter, you will further learn the implementation of TCP. The fifth chapter discusses in depth on Wide Area Network. As much as this term may be familiar, probably you do not know what it widely entails. Get a copy of this book and get to learn more on point to point services, bundle switched services, fiber optic connectivity and much more on WAN.

Finally, the last chapter of the book will take you through configuration windows servers. The author discusses relocation scenarios, the essential steps of configuring a new server and much more.

We are in the internet age, and therefore, ignorance is not an option. This book enlightens you on the basis that you should know on computer networking. Thank you for choosing this book. Please remember to leave a review on Amazon!

Chapter 1: Computer Networking

Systems interface things together. Through the USA, the gathering of streets involves putting down a system where cars can meet at one point. The reason for a system of streets is to allow individuals to effectively move to start with one spot then onto the next. PC systems comprise of interconnected PC frameworks. The motivation behind systems administration these parts together are to share data and processing assets. The internet is an obvious case of a PC network where many people get internet and computer assets throughout the world. A huge number of people who use these assets do not know how they are made as well as how they are made accessible to them. While everything is considered, that is the work of a computer jockey or the system overseer. Framework and system executives possess the assignment of guaranteeing that PC assets stay accessible. While the undertakings of these two particular jobs regularly cover, it is the activity of the system head to guarantee that PCs and other devoted system gadgets, for example, repeaters, extensions, switches, and application servers, stay interconnected. To achieve this errand, the network executive should be comfortable with the product and equipment utilized to successfully interface the different segments. In this nature, the idea of the system types and models.

Types of System

In computer networks, there are various terminologies that we have encountered. These involve the Local Area Network (LAN), Wide Area Network (WAN), Campus Area Network (CAN), and Metropolitan Area Network (MAN).

Local Area Network (LAN)

LANs include many connected hubs which are in a similar structure. A hub is any gadget which can be arranged, similar to a PC (frequently alluded as the framework), a copier, a machine, as well as a discovery gadget. It ought to be noticed that with the appearance of layer 2 steerings. The thought that the hubs inside a LAN must be topographically close winds up false.

Advantages of LAN

Benefits of sharing devices: Devices such as printers, flash disks, modems, and hard disks are inserted to assist in productivity. With these, there are minimal costs that you can incur in buying pieces of equipment.

Program sharing-With LAN, you can share the same programming on a system. One does not need to buy different programs for every system. This makes it affordable.

Easy straightforward and affordable messaging: Information can be sent over different computers. This makes it fast and affordable.

Integrated information: The data of all the clients in the system can be stored within the hard disk. Therefore, a client can still use any workstation and still get their information. Through the networks, every person can access information no matter which computer they are using as long as it is interconnected.

Data safety: Data is stored centrally on the server computer. Therefore, the information is secure since it is not difficult to oversee the information.

Network Sharing: Local Area Network offers the workplace the ability to share alone web relationship with all the LAN customers. In a cyber cafe, a single web affiliation sharing structure enables the sustainability of more affordable web costs.

Drawbacks of LAN

High installation costs: Although the LAN will do without the expense due to shared assets, on the other hand, the cost of installing LAN is high.

Security infringement: There is an option for the LAN manager to check information records for each LAN client.

Also, there can be a review of the web and computer use history of the client.

Security risk: Customers who are not authorized can access important information when the server is not verified well. The LAN head needs to make sure that there is proper verification.

LAN repairs: A LAN administrator should do repairs on the issues that come up regarding programming or PC.

Spreads a small area: A Local Area Network does not cover a huge area. It is limited to one office or one structure. A small area in an organization.

Wide Area Network (WAN)

The Wide Area Network (WAN) is a get together of organized and geologically divergent centers. As often as possible, the genuine difference between a Local Area Network and a Wide Area Network is the usage of some sort of quick media to bring together the center points. Such media joins microwave, satellite, and the broadcast. WAN is an extraordinarily wide term that is routinely associated with aggregations of LANs and various WANs similarly as gatherings of center points. One model is the Internet, which is constantly depicted as a WAN; the Internet joins the two LANs and WANs.

Strengths of WAN

It extends into a wide region as long as the business can interface on one system.

It has programming and reserves with partner operating stations.

Information can be passed very fast to some other person on the framework. This information can have images and associations. Excessive things, such as printers to the internet can be shared among all the computers on the system without getting an optional periphery for each of the computers.

Comparable data can be used by everyone on the system. It keeps up a vital good ways from issues where a couple of customers may have more prepared information than others.

Weaknesses of Wide Area Network

It needs a firewall to constrain uncontrollable from coming in and disquieting the framework.

Building a framework can be exorbitant, sluggish and bewildered. For a valuable framework, it becomes more expensive.

At the point when set up, keeping up a framework is a throughout the day work which requires sort out boss and specialists to be used.

Security is a primary issue when a wide scope of people can use information from various PCs. Protection from software engineers and contaminations incorporates more noteworthy multifaceted nature and cost.

Campus Area Network (CAN)

CAN is an interconnection of LANs and WANs. It involves the accumulation of interconnected hubs having a place with a solitary organization or college/school however whose bury association reaches out crosswise over numerous structures.

Metropolitan Area Network (MAN)

It is usually connected within the accumulation of hubs inside the territory of a metropolitan which are based under the equivalent corporate control, for example, in broadcast communications organization or free specialist organization (ISP). If you think that the LAN, WAN, MAN and CAN are posh names. You are right because they are.

Moreover, almost certainly, they will get fuzzier over the long haul and innovation develops. As a result of the fluffiness of the words, we characterize the term nearby system to mean the gathering of all hubs associated through a similar medium and having a similar system number. As it were, hubs that offer a similar system number can speak with one another without requiring the administrations of a switch.

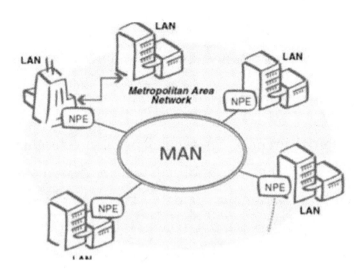

Pros of MAN

Incredibly productive and give quick correspondence using rapid transporters, for example, fiber optic links.

It gives a decent spine to the enormous system and gives more noteworthy admission to WANs.

The double transport utilized in Metropolitan Area Network assists in the transfer of information in the two headings all the while.

A MAN normally includes a few squares of a city or a whole city.

Cons of MAN

Progressively link required for a MAN association starting with one spot then onto the next.

Sometimes it is difficult to enhance security in the framework to from programmers and spying graphical districts.

Wireless Networks

Computerized remote correspondence is not another thought. Prior, Morse code was utilized to execute remote systems. Present-day advanced remote frameworks have better execution, yet the essential thought is the equivalent.

Remote can be divided into three;

Framework interconnection

Wireless Local Area Networks

Wireless Wide Area Networks

Framework Interconnection

Framework link is tied in with interlinking the segments of a PC utilizing short go radio. A few organizations got together to structure a short go remote system called Bluetooth to interface different parts, for example, screen, console, mouse, and printer, to the primary unit, without wires. Bluetooth likewise permits advanced cameras, headsets, scanners, and different gadgets to associate with a PC by just being brought inside the range.

In the most straightforward structure, framework interconnection systems utilize the ace slave idea. The framework unit is typically the ace, conversing with the mouse, console, and so forth as slaves.

Remote LANs

In this framework, there is a radio modem and reception apparatus in each Pc where it can serve at different frameworks. Remote LANs are usually winding up progressively regular in little workplaces and homes, where introducing Ethernet is viewed as an excessive amount of inconvenience. IEEE 802.11 is the standard for remote LANs, which most frameworks actualize and are also winding up across the board.

The radio system utilized for cell phones is a case of a low-transmission capacity remote WAN. This framework has effectively experienced three ages.

The original was simple and for voice, as it were.

The subsequent age was computerized and for voice, as it were.

The third era is computerized and is for both voice and information.

System Models

A system model is a reflection of an arrangement to achieve a connection between the frameworks. Also, system models are said to be system stacks. TCP/IP and Internet Package Exchange (IPX) are included in the system models. There are layers in a system model. Every layer has its full importance. There are conventions in each layer that are shown to implement assignments. A layer is a gathering of connections and comes with a certain value. There are many types of system models. They are all recognized with a specific task, for example, the TCP/IP system model. Other

OSI-RM

This is the World Wide firm for certification (ISO) which advances models. ISO started to take a blast at building up a standard for multivendor PC interconnectivity in the 1970s. The results that were spread during the 80s was the Open System Interconnection (OSI) model. The OSI model consolidates conventions which are utilized to execute a system stack. The conventions aren't utilized widely to a great extent because of the fame of the TCP/IP convention suite. Therefore, the model of OSI involves seven layers which are used mainly as a source of the perspective model, hence OSI-RM. System models are laid out in the way of OSI-RM. This is illustrated from layer 1 to layer 7.

Layer 7: Every effort of systems administration started in the submission layer. Folder move, informing, network perusing, and different applications are within the layer. Every submission will properly conjure handling information for broadcast using fine characterized layer interface under this one

Layer 6: This layer is the presentation layer. It is in charge of information organizing. It is responsible for requesting a bit and byte as well as representing a drifting point. Some of the examples include external data representation (XDR) and Abstract Syntax Notation (ASN).

Layer 5: This layer is responsible for information trading of information throughout exchange discussion conventions. This layer is to a great extent planned for the update and terminal correspondences. There is no pertinence with deference to TCP/IP networking.

Layer 4: This is the transport layer which is responsible for a solid exchange of information among frameworks. It is concerned with correspondence moment which involves; stream control, asking of data, mistake discovery and retrieving of information.

Layer 3: This is the Network layer. Its work is to convey information between various frameworks in the combined frameworks.

LAYER 2: This is the information link layer which gives guidelines for propelling as well as accepting information among two associated hubs along a specific material means.

LAYER 1: This is the physical layer that characterizes the needed equipment. This includes interfaces and cables for a specific vehicle of correspondence, for example, light-based and radiofrequency.

Along these lines, techniques for transmitting and receiving bit floods of data are characterized

Epitome and De-multiplexing

When information is transmitted from the top layer to the bottom layer, there is a specific

measure of data control that is usually connected in the information. The data in control is known as the header and it is largely included at the front of the data. A trailer is the control data attached to the information.

Not many trailers have conventions but every convention has headers. Exemplification is the procedure that involves adding headers and trailers to the information. Further, the payload is the information between the trailer and the header. Therefore, while connected, the trailer, header, and payload make up a data unit.

There involves show giving names to convention information components

Within the TCP/IP convention group: In TCP they have named sections, while in UDP and IP, they are named datagrams, further in the information connect layer, they are named outlines. Nonexclusive name parcel is usually utilized when the convention information piece does not submit to a particular convention/layer. The exemplification procedure is as follows; The procedure information element at one layer sums up the payload at the bottom layer. Every layer includes a header, Ethernet and also includes a trailer. Along these lines, there is an increase in the transparency of transmitting information from one layer to the another.

Headers as well as trailers which come from a certain layer prepared uniquely using substances at a similar layer. The header of a conveyed TCP portion is prepared distinctly using TCP convention at the host which obtains the TCP section. Every convention header information element is organized into several protocol explicit fields. The determination of a protocol is the organization of the header. The Header fields involve a foundation and a goal address, grouping numbers, payload length, and checksum for error control.

Just in case there is no fixed size in the header, then it has to be included as a header field. On the side of the beneficiary, every layer spreads from the header on that layer and goes through the payload into a convention at the top layer. Every layer has to select on to which top layer convention with which to transmit the payload. An example, Ethernet gadget host has to dole out the payload of a structure to IP or ARP. The payload of an IP datagram has to be appointed by the IP address to UDP or TCP or another convention. In this procedure of allotting of the payload to a top layer, the convention is known as demultiplexing.

Background of the internet

The beginning of the internet goes back to the late 1960s as an examination system financed by the United States Department of finance with an end goal to manufacture a correspondence system-dependent within the standards of the packet exchanges. The Advanced Research Projects Agency (ARPANET) was the system at first. By the mid -the 1970s, the rise of a few businesses and those, not businesses parcel exchanging systems, and the advancement of different networking technologies, for example, bundle radio and neighborhood, made a need to interconnect("internetwork") various kinds of systems through a typical convention design. The advancement of TCP, which at the beginning involved the engagement of TCP and IP at the 1970s addressed the issue through giving a convention which is in support of webwork, that utilizes a wide range of advancements while also possessed with various associations. The phrase "the Internet" was utilized to allude to the arrangement of every TCP and IP web works with an of all TCP/IP based internetworks with a familiar address. The TCP and IP convention engineering started taking root and shape in the 1980s which had also turned into the convention ARPANET standard. All through in the 80s, system frameworks of TCP/IP rose that joined colleges and registering focuses, and furthermore crossing point to the current ARPANET. The NSFNET system built by the National Science Foundation turned into ARPANET's heir as the Internet's central foundation. In the late 1980s, numerous provincial and worldwide TCP/IP based systems associated with the NSFNET, and made the establishment for the present worldwide Internet framework in the 1980s. Recently, the web comprises of numerous thousand, for the most part, business, joined together and gives system administrations. The sensational development of the web.

The Internet Framework

The Internet Framework The framework of the Internet comprises of an organization of associated systems that are each independently overseen. The systems are composed in a loose-fitting order, where the quality "free" alludes to the way that the progression isn't needed, yet has developed to its current structure. At the bottom layer in the chain of importance are concealed systems, which are either campus or corporate systems, as well as nearby internet specialist organizations (ISPs). Regional systems are in the next layer which involves the inclusion of one or a few states. At the top degree of the order are spine systems which range whole nations or even mainlands. The regional networks, ISPs, as well as spine systems are additionally named, individually, Tier 1,2 and 3 network specialist organizations (NSPs).

In the United States of America, Local ISPs, corporate systems, and ISPs are commonly associated with at least one regional network or, less frequently, to a spine organize. There are less than twenty tier-1 NSPs, fewer than 100 tier 2 NSPs as well as thousands of tier-3 ISPs. Point-of-Presence (POP) is the area where a corporate network gets admission into the net. On the other hand, where spine systems and regional networks join to trade. Peering is supposed to be accessible either as open peering or private peering. Open peering often happens at devoted areas, named Internet trade focuses (IXPs), and these are where a huge number of systems change their traffic. On the other hand, in private peering, two systems build up a straight connection to one another. The inward

system and gear of every system of the Internet are self-sufficient. The system topology of a nearby ISP may comprise just of few routers, a couple of modem banks for the dial-in clients, and an entrance connect to a local system. The internal structure of a spine system is essentially increasingly perplexing and delineates the system topology. Every hub of the system topology is a network by itself, with an enormous arrangement of systems administration gear. The depicted gadgets are a switch or different bits of system gear, and every bolt speaks to an outgoing system interface. Just a few connections associate with different hubs of the same backbone system, and most connections interface with different systems or to clients.

Organization and Standard Bodies of the Internet

Organization and Standard Bodies of the Internet Numerous managerial bodies regulate and deal with the development of the internet. Based on the foundation of the internet, the organization of the Internet depends on collaboration and illustrated by at least focal control. The Internet Society (ISOC) is a universal philanthropic expert association that provides regulatory internet assistance. ISOC was established in 1992 and serves as the hub for the institutionalization of the internet assortments. Internet Architecture Board (IAB) involves a specialized warning gathering of the Internet Society, it gives architecture supervision of the architecture to the conventions and the institutionalization procedure. A gathering to organize the improvement of fresh conventions and gauges is called the Internet Engineering Task Force (IETF). The IETF is sorted out in gatherings of work which are distributed to a particular theme. These work gatherings record their effort in statements, which are named Request for Comments (RFCs), which also are the for internet benchmarks. Everything about the internet conventions is distributed as RFCs. An example, instance, IP is indicated in

RFC791, TCP in RFC 793, ARP in RFC 826, and much more. The little division of the distributed RFCs is aligned to progress toward becoming Internet principles. Web measures are said to be experiencing a lot of phases, ranging from the draft to the accepted standard, draft standard, and finally the standard of the internet. The endorsed RFCs Internet guidelines are doled out with the STD record. Currently, there include as much as 61 designated standards of the internet. A significant Organization of the internet piece comprises of the task and for seeing of one of a kind identifiers. These incorporate area terms, IP addresses, the port numbers such as the web servers, protocol numbers which are used for demultiplexing. Since the start of ARPANET till the part of the arrangement organization of identifiers was finished by a solitary individual who is Jon Postel. The privatization of the internet has prompted an arrangement where identifiers are overseen by associations with wide universal support. Currently, Internet Corporation for Assigned Names (ICANN) accepts the accountability for the work of specialized convention factors, distribution including the spread of IP address space, the board of the area name framework, and others. The administration of IP

address and space name allocation isn't finished by ICANN itself, yet by associations that are approved by ICANN. The ICANN has conceded minimal Regional Internet Registries (RIRs) which is the expert to assign IP addresses inside specific land zones. Currently, RIRs are three in number. They include; Asia Pacific Network Information Center (APNIC) which is for the district of ASIA, the Reseaux IP Europeens Network Coordination Center (RIPE NCC) which serves Europe and surrounding areas. The third is American Registry for Internet Numbers (ARIN) which is for the sub-Saharan Africa and Americans. The spread of area terms is finished using an enormous private association, that is authorized by ICANN. An important assignment of ICANN in the location term is the starting of new to level spaces like Edu, US, and JP.

Advantages and disadvantages of the internet

Current life has turned out to be simpler and the individuals of the world need to gratitude to the huge commitment of web innovation to correspondence and data sharing. There is no uncertainty that the web has caused our life to end up simpler and progressively helpful. We can utilize the web to speak with individuals around the globe, working together by utilizing the web, make another companion and know various societies, scanning for data, examining and so on. The web takes into consideration correspondence through email as well as guarantees simple accessibility of data, pictures, and items in addition to other things. Consistently the web keeps on giving another office, something new that is enormously helpful and that makes life simpler for web clients. In any case, the web likewise contains some undesirable components or detriments. Coming up next are the focal points and inconveniences of the web. The internet has brought about numerous advantages in the world. We list them below.

Advantages

Initially, the web can give an individual a chance to speak with individuals in essentially any pieces of the world through the web or email, without leaving his room. Email enabled people groups to speak with at least occasions. It is presently possible to make an impression on any pieces of the world through a basic email address and the message is conveyed in merely seconds. Each organization is utilizing email in business. The accommodation of email has enabled organizations to grow and speaks with their merchants and clients found everywhere throughout the world in records times. Individual correspondence has likewise turned out to be simpler gratitude to email. Talk rooms, video conferencing are the absolute most recent augmentations in this innovation and these have enabled people groups to visit continuously. Additionally, there is a great deal of errand people benefits in advertising. With the assistance of such benefits, it has turned out to be exceptionally simple to build up a sort of worldwide companionship where you can share your contemplations and investigate different societies. The web additionally enables individuals inside an association to effectively impart and share data.

Second, data is most likely the greatest favorable circumstances that the web offers. The web is a virtual fortunes trove of data. Any sorts of data on any point under the sun are accessible on the web. The web indexes like Google, Yahoo are at your administration through the web. There is a tremendous measure of data accessible on the web for pretty much every subject known to man, running from government law and administrations, exchange fairs and meetings, showcase data, new thoughts, and specialized help, the rundowns are perpetual. We can utilize these web search tools, sites committed to various subjects and countless articles and papers are accessible for examination in a matter of a couple of moments.

Gatherings on various destinations enable people groups to talk about and share their considerations and data with others situated at better places everywhere throughout the world. Regardless of whether this data is the most recent news happenings on the planet or data about your preferred VIP, everything is accessible readily available. An immense reserve of information is accessible on the web on every subject. With this storage facility of data, individuals can expand their insight bank as well as can do as such without burning through their time through customary methods, for example, visiting libraries and directing comprehensive research. With the web, understudies can spare their occasions to scan for data and utilizing their opportunity to do different works.

This is especially pertinent for understudies who can utilize this abundance of data for their school undertakings and furthermore adapt new things about the subjects they are keen on. Truth be told, this web is for some schools and colleges that are presently ready to dole out activities and work to the understudies and pursues their advancement which can be effectively posted on the school or college inside sites. Online training has developed at an exceptionally quick pace since the web permits the advancement and employments of imaginative instruments for giving instruction. College understudies and teachers can convey through the web. Moreover, a few colleges are likewise contributions far separations courses to cause concentrate to turn out to be progressively wasteful and accommodation. The web turns into an entryway for the individuals who need to adapt however can't bear the cost of the living charges at remote nations.

Thirdly, excitement is another well-known motivation behind why numerous individuals want to surf the web. Truth be told, the web has turned out to be very fruitful in catching the multifaceted media outlet. Downloading games or simply surfing the VIP sites are a portion of the utilizations individuals have found. Indeed, even VIPs are utilizing the web viably for limited time crusades. Other than that, various games can be downloaded for nothing. The business of web-based gaming has tasted emotional and extraordinary considerations by game darlings. The web has likewise reformed the diversions business. Individuals these days no compelling reason to go to a film corridor to watch your preferred motion picture. Rather than watching motion pictures at the film presently have organizations offering their administrations where you simply can download or arrange your preferred motion picture and watch it with a quick web association. Other than that, you additionally can download other significant programming or your preferred music in a matter of a couple of minutes. Various shareware programs enable you to share and download your preferred music and recordings. The web additionally permits individuals from various societies and foundation to associate with one another. Web gaming is a tremendous business and enables excited gamers to contend with one another in games notwithstanding when they are situated far separated. Moreover, dating has additionally enabled individuals to locate their forthcoming perfect partners.

Through the web, shopping has likewise got a total makeover because of the commitments of the web. You have numerous sites selling an assortment of items on the web and one simply need to choose or offer for the ideal item and whole money related exchanges can be led through the web. Online business has an office given the web and whole worldwide business arrangements can be directed over the web. The move of cash is additionally no longer multiple times devouring occupation and with only a tick of a catch, you can undoubtedly move assets to wherever you wish. A portion of these administrations of courses include some significant downfalls. The web has made life exceptionally helpful. With various online administrations, you would now be able to play out the entirety of your exchange on the web. You can books tickets for a film, move reserves, pay service bills, charges and so forth, and appropriate from your home. Some movement sites even arrangement a schedule according to your inclinations and deals with carrier tickets, inn reservation, and so forth by utilizing the web, shoppers can think about the costs of the item before settling on choices to buy.

Individuals who accept that the effects of the web on understudies are positives said that web help understudies by giving them convenient material and assets for their investigations. It is a major reality that now understudies takes a great deal of assistance from the web. Understudies have any issue in regards to their examinations or the day by day life they can discover heaps of answers for that issue from the web. There they can discover articles of researcher and other expert individuals which would be useful for them. They can take addresses from various scholastics on various subjects.

One of the most significant advantages of the web is that understudies can acquire from the web through bloggers. Understudies can check out gaining through the web. It would be an incredible wellspring of salary for them and furthermore, it would give them a major encounter of composing. The understudies who are keen on media and needed to be an essayist, later on, must do this work. This would expand their expert abilities which would lead them towards an incredible future.

Understudies can likewise utilize the web for social availability and there are bunches of internet-based life sites which for the most part understudies use for interpersonal interaction. For example, Facebook, Twitter, Weibo and so forth are the celebrated person to person communication site. Understudies can get in touch with themselves with remote understudies and talk about them on the diverse issue to improve their abilities and learning. By utilizing web astutely, understudies can get much data to enhance their insight.

Disadvantages of the internet

Be that as it may, for every one of its preferences and positive viewpoints, the web has its dull and terrible side as well. The ongoing bits of gossip that mongering about racial uproars in Kuala Lumpur which in made a tumult, just demonstrates how this apparatus, with its unparalleled notoriety as data deaths and friends notorieties, can endure if web offices are manhandled, particularly by those with a grievance.

Other than that, a few understudies will invest an excess of energy in the web. Understudies are probably going to disregard their investigations. On the off chance that the motion picture has too solid a hold, even old individuals are probably going to disregard a portion of their significant work. Understudies may lose focus on their examinations since they invested a lot of energy on the web. Some of them cannot even separate their opportunity to do schoolwork yet they invested their energy in viewing a motion picture or talking with their companions through the web.

While the web has made life simpler for individuals from multiple points of view it is additionally mirroring an uglier side to its reality through various issues that it has hurled for its clients. With a lot of data uninhibitedly accessible on the web burglary and abuse of this data is a reasonable plausibility. Over and over you see instances of individuals utilizing another person's data and research and passing it off as their own. Kids these days appear losing their capacity to speak with others. They are utilized to speak with others utilizing the web however they can't speak with others face by a face familiar. It was an abnormal sight that the web needed to make individuals losing their capacity to convey. It is because individuals presently are over-relying upon the web.

Another issue or impediment of the web is that it has enabled a lot of namelessness to countless individuals who may get to the various sites, gatherings and visit rooms accessible. This has enabled distorted people to on occasion exploit blameless individuals and misuse their trust. We can generally get notification from the news that con artists utilized the web to make wrongdoings. The con artists will warm up to single women and cheat them by utilizing sweet words. Forlorn single women in all respects effectively get in the snare of these con artists. These miscreants regularly will swindle these women to bank-in cash to them. A portion of the con artists attempts to acquire cash from these women.

There are a large group of games that are accessible on the web and this has made most youngsters evade all outside action. Without physical movement, youngsters can undoubtedly fall prey to many ways of life-related infections, for example, stoutness, aside from neglecting to create relational abilities. Aside from these elements, sitting consistently before a PC screen can genuinely harm our eyes, and put a strain on our neck and shoulders. Youngsters are in their creating years and these elements can make deep-rooted issues for them. Kids will turn out to be more viciousness because influenced by web games. There are such a large number of web games that contain viciousness substance and it might influence a negative impact on kids.

Another weakness of the web is destructive to little kids. Youngsters these days are investigated to the web and they are utilized to keep up the web as their day by day life. This is perhaps the best danger web postures to kids. The web has given a simple medium to kids to access sex entertainment and this can make them either become explicitly freak or explicitly addictive. This wonder has additionally caused another issue, and that is the expansion in the pervasiveness of explicitly transmitted sicknesses (STD) in kids. As indicated by reports, one out of each four adolescents gets tainted with an STD consistently. The grown-up substance that is available on the web advances flippant sex and makes false thoughts in the psyches of understudies.

If you have been following news of late, at that point, you should comprehend what we are alluding to. Kids have been baited by pedophiles acting like great Samaritans and have been physically mishandled and attacked. The web has additionally made it simple for deceitful components to connect with kids and this has prompted an expansion in the instances of capturing and character burglaries. About 60% youthful adolescents in the United States have confessed to reacting to messages from outsiders. This sort of conduct is amazingly dangerous and has made youngsters incredibly helpless against becoming casualties of digital wrongdoing.

Conclusion

The focuses referenced above have presented new difficulties to educators and guardians. There are requests from different quarters that there ought to be a type of guideline to check this issue. In any case, we accept that as opposed to making the web an unthinkable, we ought to instruct youngsters to utilize it for their advantage. It is fitting for guardians to screen how much time their youngsters spend on the web, and if conceivable set a period point of confinement till which they would be permitted to utilize the web. Having the PC in the parlor rather than a tyke's room can likewise guarantee control on what they are getting to on the web. It is likewise significant that you converse with them about 'sexual intimacy supposing that you don't converse with them, they will go to their companions and web for answers which may not give bona fide data. Guardians assume a significant job in this substance and they need to focus on their kids in spite of them get influenced by the web.

Despite the fact that reviews on this issue are in fundamental stages, it has been built up that youngsters who invest a large portion of their energy in the web, demonstrate a curious sort of conduct which is set apart by a desire to be on the web constantly, so much that the kid may demonstrate all exercises and become inundated in the virtual world. Studies led throughout the years have discovered that a great many people who experience the ill effects of Internet dependence issue are youthful grown-ups, who effectively fall into the draw of investigating everything accessible on the web. In America alone, it has been assessed that around 10-15 million individuals are experiencing web compulsion issue, and this is expanding at the pace of 25% consistently. The web had controlled some of them who are depending on the web in their life exercises. A large portion of them will get distraught if they can't interface with the web. It turns into a sort of physiology affliction around us.

The web concentrated on the negative impacts, it not the slightest bit implies that we are undermining the significance of web in our lives. We have composed this article for the web group of spectators, and you are understanding it through the web, which itself clarifies the positive side of web use. It is for us to choose whether we use innovation for the advancement of our lives or put it to unabated maltreatment. Youngsters may not be developed enough to get this, yet us as guardians, educators and watchmen need to guarantee that we instill the correct conduct in our kids. In conclusion, we need to take the duties to guide out kids to utilize web carefully and guarantee them to get the right data from the web.

Addresses and Numbers

While at the systems administration model where we experienced many various location systems: such as port numbers, MAC addresses and domain names. It is good to understand that space terms, the IP locations, as well as and MAC locations have not been redirected to switches, however, it is done in their system edges. And because many clients chip away at the host including a solitary system edge, the qualification among the system and host is sometimes not important. This becomes distinctive during working with switches. The addresses of Media Access Control (MAC) are usually utilized to assign arrange edges at the information connection level. The casing of header to differentiate the source and goal of an edge is done by MAC addresses. Utilization of addresses is not a must for every information connection layer. Example, in case two switches are joined at each point connection, for example, a fast sequential connection, there would be no compelling reason to make use of addresses in an edge to recognize the goal. Each edge that is broadcasted at the far end of each point connection goes to the gadget at the opposite part of the bargain. Along these lines, the propelling from one point to another in a frame connection is aware of where the edge is heading to, as well as point to point connection recipient of a casing realizes that the casing propeller is the gadget at the opposite part of the arrangement of information connection levels for point-to-point connections, of which don't utilize addresses for network interfaces.

Within a neighborhood, numerous system interface gets to communicate broadcast channel, where it assumes the job of a mutual connection. Every broadcast on the mutual connection can be gotten through all organized borders joined to the common connection. Accordingly, each system interface must have a one of a kind location, and each broadcasted edge must convey a goal source address. With the goal, the address is required with the goal that a system interface that gets an edge within the shared connection can decide whether it is the expected recipient of the edge. The outline header is the host of the source header. Many neighborhoods embrace a location conspire that was created by the IEEE 802committee, an institutionalization body that has characterized numerous gauges for the neighborhood, token ring, Ethernet and Local area networks. A piece of the MAC level is the location plan. In this plan, MAC addresses or equipment locations are 48 bits in length.

The show for MAC documentation will in general use the hexadecimal report, whereby each byte is a colon or a dash confined. 01110001. The address for the MAC framework interface card is interminable and is apportioned when the card is made. Every framework interface card gets a globally unique MAC address. Right when the system interface card of a host is displaced, the host is come to through the other MAC address. Since starting late, some framework interface cards enable to modify the MAC address of a framework interface card. In any case, changing the MAC address of a framework interface card may achieve area duplication. Thusly, when the MAC address is a balanced assurance that the doled out MAC address is unique in the area organized. The errand of the MAC address space is coordinated by the IEEE. Every association that produces organize interface cards gets address discourages from the IEEE as an a24-bit prefix. The producer uses this prefix for the underlying 24 bits of the MAC locations of its organizing interface cards. The last 24 bits are apportioned by

the maker, who must guarantee that the bits are consigned without duplication.

At the point when the area square is drained, the producer can request another area discourage from the IEEE. Note, in any case, that one24-piece prefix continues for

224^a 16.7 million interface cards. A captivating aftereffect of this task plan is

that the MAC address can be used to recognize the creator of an Ethernet card. For the MAC addresses in Section 1, we can affirm that the organize interface card of Argon and Neon were created by the 3COM Company, since the prefixes 00:21:af is consigned to the 3COM Company, and that the Ethernet interface of the switch with MAC address 00:e0:f8:24:a9:20 was made by Cisco Systems. Apart from than recognizing the creator, the area space of MAC areas is level, implying that MAC areas try not to encode any pecking request or other structure that can be abused for the transport of edges. There are two or three one of a kind areas. The area ff:ff: that is, the location with every one of the 48 bits set to '1', is appointed as conveying address. A packaging where the goal address is the conveyed area is sent to all framework contraptions on the close by region arrange. For example, the Ethernet traces that pass on the ARP request packs have the objective location set to the conveyed location. Addresses where the underlying 24 bits are reset to 01:00:5e is multicast MAC addresses.

Port numbers

Port numbers At the drive layer, TCP and UDP use 16-piece port numbers to perceive an application procedure, which is either an application-layer show or an application program. Each TCP area or UDP datagram passes on the port number of the source and the objective in the bundle header. The IP address, the vehicle show number (0x60 for TCP, 0x11 for

UDP), and the port number of a group strikingly perceive a methodology on the Web. Right when a bundle is gotten by the vehicle layer, the vehicle show number and the port number give the demultiplexing data to enable the data to the correct technique. Since the amount of the vehicle convention is used in the demultiplexing decision, a host can have ports for TCP furthermore, ports for UDP with a similar number. For example, a UDP port 80 and a TCP port 80 are segregated ports, which that can be bound different application forms. Most framework organizations and application programs on the Web have client assistance communication. When allocating port numbers the server tasks of the client-server applications are allocated to without a doubt comprehended port number, inferring that all hosts on the Internet have default port numbers for their server programs. For example, the eminent port number for an HTTP server is port 80, and the extraordinary port amounts of various applications are port 21 for File Transfer Protocol (FTP) servers, port 25 for the mail servers that run the Simple Mail Transfer Protocol (SMTP), and port 23 for Telnet servers. All extraordinary port numbers are in the range from 0 to 1023. The errand of unquestionably comprehended port numbers to the server undertakings of utilization layer conventions is, generally, set away in a record on a host. The errand can be found in RFC 1700 (STD2). The advantage of using comprehended port numbers is that client ventures of utilization layer conventions which need to get to a server program can get the port number of the server essentially utilizing an area query. The errand of port numbers 1024 and higher isn't coordinated. Port numbers in this range are utilized by client tasks of framework organizations. All things considered, client undertakings apportion a port number just for a brief time allotment furthermore, release the port number when the client program has finished its task. Due to the transient circulation, port numbers at least 1024 are called transient port numbers. At the point when making programming for application undertakings and application layer shows for the Internet, engineers, for the most part, use the connection application programming interface. A connection provides for the application designer a reflection that resembles that of a record. An application program can open a connection, and a while later read from also, stay in contact with an attachment, and, when a task is done, close a connection. My accomplice (definitive) a connection to a port number, an application program gets to the Internet address space.

IP Addresses

The identifier of a framework edge at the system level is known as the IP address.

At the point when the net crossing point is associated with the Internet, then there should be an all-round IP address special inside the location position of the Internet. Then this means that there are no two system interfaces on the Internet that can own similar IP addresses. Every gadget associated with the web has an extraordinary identifier. Most systems currently, which include many PCs on the web, utilize TCP/IP as a typical to impart the system. IP Address is one of a kind identifier within the TCP/IP. The two sorts of IP Addresses areIPv6 and IPv4. IPv4 versus IPv6 IPv4 utilizes 32 parallel bits to make a solitary remarkable location

on the system. four numbers isolated by spots communicate an IPv4 address. Every number is a base 10 for the decimal portrayal in an eight-digit parallel (base-2) number, additionally called an octet. IPv6 utilizes 128 twofold bits to make a solitary one of a kind location on the system. An IPv6 address is communicated by eight gatherings of hexadecimal (base-16) numbers isolated by colons. Gatherings of numbers that contain every one of the zeros are regularly discarded to spare space, leaving a colon separator to stamp the hole. IPv6 space is a lot bigger than the IPv4 space due to the utilization of hexadecimal just as having 8 gatherings. Most gadgets use IPv4. Be that as it may, because of the approach of IoT gadgets and the more noteworthy interest for IP Addresses, an ever-increasing number of gadgets are tolerating IPv6.

Protocols of the Application layer

The importance of transfer reports between the computers, have access to resource enrollment and assist customer correspondence at separate hosts, was looked at by the first of internet apps from the late 1960s and mid-1970s. The apps that discussed the following problems: In the integral countless extended periods of the Web, FTP, Telnet, and Email were the mind-boggling programs. The World Wide Web's rise in the mid-1990s rapidly produced the most normal Internet application browsing the internet. Lately, applications for streaming audio and video, interaction across the Web, and suitable exchanging of files have once again changed the names of Online apps. This chapter describes information on the online functionality of apps and also how apps manipulate the web to provide service-clients with context organizations. This is based on the surface of the Earth, along with area and ocean areas, which are approximately 196,935,000 square miles in size. Multiple Web apps which are centered on application-layer displays that the IETF has institutionalized them. Around it, we quickly undoubtedly portray the most common app layer on the net, in which we focus onto the application protocols used in the Website Lab. Because this manuscript and the Online Lab core demonstrates on web errands, and thus less on how apps use web, we wouldn't address it all about the apps and application layer displays. But at the other side, we may give a template which the usage layer reveals strategy, concentrating onto the communications among app initiatives and what the app layer demonstrates, as well as between what app layer shows and transport layer. Taking a look for at this goal, we find a few resemblances that what different application layer displays.

File Transfer

Amongst the most proven application layer displays is the File Transfer Protocol (FTP) for recurring documents between PC systems and it was created prior to the actual TCP / IP display suite. FTP is a client server that shows where the Ftp server receives the FTP server. The Ftp server justifies itself for setting up an FTP meeting with a client name and a hidden phrase. Enticing the verification results in the establishment of an FTP meeting in which the Ftp server can upload and exchange files and record documents. FTP recognizes the possession and access benefits of the records when transferring the documents. Most of them had a service system, all things regarded, just like FTP, that provides a smart query row functionality to operate an FTP session. This service system is used in all parts of the Online Lab. FTP customers can participate distinct apps, such as internet projects, in the same way. Ambiguous FTP is a notable type of record transfer regime that encourages the system to record on an FTP server. The Ftp server can set up a unique FTP meeting by providing the client name "dark" and an obligatory secret word (the FTP server, as a rule of thumb, asks to provide a mail address as a secret phrase).

FTP utilizes TCP because its car shows to ensure a reliable exchange in transferred data. With each FTP meeting, two TCP allegiances are created, called command membership and data membership. Power membership can be used for user captions and client emails. The information association will be used for the register unit. The Ftp client utilizes the influential TCP harbour 21 for power association, and the noteworthy TCP gateway 20 for information association, and the Ftp server selects the accessible temporary port figures. The power allegiance is arranged across the start of the FTP meeting and will remain awake throughout the meeting's life time. The command membership will be used by the Ftp server for checking, for establishing unique meeting variables, and for downloading or transferring files. The information allegiance is opened and closed for each movement of a file or report. The information membership is shut at the stage where a paper or document review has also been transferred. The information affiliation will be certainly-opened when there is another file move. As usual, the information affiliation is created by the Ftp client upon request. The Ftp server begins a TCP server that conveys the port code of this device to the command linked to the FTP server for a connection on a fleeting port. Once the signal is received by the Ftp client, it can demand the FTP client associated information. FTP safety pressure has been that the title of the client, as well as the secret key displayed by the FTP client in the power partnership across the start of the FTP session, are not encoded. Consequently, anyone with the capacity to capture requests from the Ftp server can have the title of the client as well as the hidden name used by Ftp server. The Ftp server puts wheels to both the FTP server, and the Ftp client responds with such a three-digit reaction system and an explanatory message. The Ftp server handles as well as the Ftp client answers are transferred as ASCII characters. The portion of the action query as well as the part of the agreement reaction is discussed by the part of the agreement, that involves the ASCII outstanding personalities Carriage Return (ASCII10) followed by Row Feed (ASCII 13). Essentially once the TCP connection with the TCP harbour 21 of the Ftp client is created, the Ftp client gives an obvious indication that it will be set up to join forces for the next FTP meeting. In the meantime, the client provides the title of the client and the description of the puzzle. When the verification is efficient, the client will submit the IP address as well as the container code of the temporary ship to the information membership. The Domain name and the submission quantity is sent to the affected citation record, in which the preceding four digits indicate the IP address and last two digits show the transaction amount.

The Trivial Transfer protocol (TFTP)

The Trivial File Transfer Protocol (TFTP) is an unimportant display for shifting documents without identification without packet headers as in FTP. TFTP is regularly utilized by devices without an unchanging limit with regards to recreating a fundamental memory picture remote server bootstrap when the systems are checked. In the absence of any safety, that use of TFTP is usually limited. TFTP utilizes a hazardous vehicle to display UDP for information conveyance. Every TFTP text is transmitted in an alterative UDP packet headers. The two bytes underpinning the TFTP signal show the type of message that can be a permission to upload an file, a purchases to migrate a history, a information text, or a assertion or amble text. A TFTP meeting is started if a TFTP user starts sending a request to leave or install a record from either a short UDP station to the (excellent) UDP harbor 69 of both the TFTP server. The TFTP provider selects its special vaporous UDP channel right after the application is received and utilizes this channel to speak to the TFTP server. In the same way, the temporary devices are used by both client and client.

Because UDP may not retrieve lost or demolished information, TFTP is responsible for maintaining the exchange of information integrity. TFTP transfers information in 512 byte blocks. A 2-byte lengthy collection amount is assigned to each square and is transferred in an alternative UDP packet headers. Once sending the associated space, a circle must be viewed. The block is transmitted electronically just when accreditation is not obtained before a countdown ends. Just as the agency receives a block that is below 512 lines of code long, it considers the deal's piece to arrive.

Remote Login

To execute captions on a distant server, Remote Login Telnet is a remote login display. The Telnet conference keeps running in a customer-server manner and utilizes the data transfer TCP display. A customer starts a Telnet meeting by reaching a distant user on a Telnet server. Such as FTP, Telnet's manifestations returned to the early ARPANET throughout the late 1960s. Coming early, Telnet's use in accessible structures has also been weakened as Telnet will not give amazing affirmations to strangers who can view ("snoop") communications between a Telnet user and a Telnet server. A personality produced on the comforting does not appear on-screen on the Telnet server, irrespective of it being transcribed as an ASCII personality and distributed to a distant Telnet server. The character ASCII is viewed on the server just as a client produced the character on the distant machine's convenience. Throughout the event that the mouse click notices any return, this output is represented as a product (ASCII) and sent to the Telnet server on their screen. The output can only be the formed feature (resonance of the) or it could be the output of a display performed on a distant Telnet server. For transactions, Telnet utilizes a simple TCP connection. The Telnet server utilizes the outstanding TCP harbour 23 as well as a transitory TCP port is used by the Telnet customer. The Telnet server and user assembles a ton of variables for the Telnet meeting in the aftermath of setting up the TCP membership, such as node type, line velocity, at any point characters can or can not reverberate to the customer, etc. However the Telnet user puts one TCP part of each created character if by any possibility that a Telnet session is expressly organized to not do so. Telnet provides some chance by tracing information from the distinction of equipment and programming in servers and regards a virtual contraction called Network Virtual Terminal (NVT). The Telnet user and Telnet server trace engagement to the ASCII file name from a reassurance and return to a display. It is now

45

encrypted as an ASCII character when a personality is sent through the structure. In addition, the friendly host converts the personality and deciphers it into community personality layout whenever an ASCII image is passed on to the TCP panel. Rlogin is an optional distant login software that runs the Unix operating system for servers. Rlogin abuses the manner the user and server operate an equal working structure and is clearer than Telnet in this sense. Surge is an app system on distant Unix to execute a single request. Similarly, there is also an app program called RCP for file transfers around Unix. In either scenario, this social occurrence of uses includes bad safety and is therefore frequently weakened. The Safe Casing display package provides application layer services for distant check-in and file movement organizations comparable to FTP, Telnet, rlogin, rsh, and RCP, yet guarantees safely recorded communications between unreliable organizations. All Safe Shell parts provide identification, safety and authenticity of information, using a range of estimates of encoding and authentication, and ensure the safety or reliability of intersections among users against normal ambushes. Safe Casing continues to operate over a TCP membership on the Web as a client-server convention, and Safe Shell applications using the notable TCP interface 22.

WEB

Developed in the mid-1990s, the World wide web is another Internet-based application for access to the substance. Within a couple of years, the Web became the most influential Web apps, and web apps have outmatched users on the Net. The Web is a dispersed framework of html that is understood as an implementation for customer support. Domain controller transactions are recovered and displayed by a web client scheme called an online program. By use of Hypertext Markup Language (HTML), the stories give an indication occasionally that the websites are structured. HTML documents are substance reports containing HTML marks that show how the content should seem in a web program's UI. A hyperlink is a tag of a distinctive kind. It is a connection to the next document that can be set up on an alternative Browser. Hyperlinks could be prompted with such a keyboard shortcut straight once appearing in a system. The system reinvests the record mentioned in the link when it starts. A internet system supports a mixture of documents on distinct servers that allude to each other via links, thus providing clients a sense of researching a global study library. Analogous to a Uniform Resource Locator (URL), the territory of a study is transmitted onto the Internet. A URL shows a beautiful region for just a internet study. It can mention an HTML document, but it is contiguous to whichever distinct documents a internet system can get to.

HTTP

The Hypertext Transfer Protocol (HTTP) is the Web app
element display. HTTP is indeed a reaction display of concern
in which an HTTP user provides requests to such an HTTP
server and the HTTP server reacts with status data, potentially
requested by an HTML file. HTTP employs TCP for
information motion and an exceptional TCP interface 80 is
used by the HTTP server to recognize TCP registration
requests. HTTP is a self-governing display because the HTTP
server may not maintain customers executable code about
such a query. Every HTTP server treats a user requests
publicly, owing little attention of whether a comparable client
makes different resulting requests. So there is no meeting
thinking like in Telnet and FTP. An HTTP client starts one
TCP connection for each sale to the HTTP server in
progressively ready kinds of HTTP that are still being used
currently. Only when the user asks the HTTP server
differently, the amount of TCP connection between the HTTP
user and the HTTP server can increase enormously. In order
to bring down the number of TCP associations, HTTP/1.1, the
current variability of HTTP, the licensing of various HTTP
sales and the reaction to a comparison TCP association
abandon the TCP affiliation open until the application has
been made. Before issuing fresh requirements, the HTTP user
doesn't need to keep up until sales are completed. As with
different many web software layer displays, HTTP signals are

transferred as ASCII material using action development bit to display the strategy section. A customer's only well-known HTTP posts are HTML applications or different accounts. Whether the client reacts with a message containing the quoted record or, if the requesting can't be satisfied, with a mix-up code.

Chapter 2: Storage Architecture

A few strategies for putting away information have developed to adapt to the prerequisite to save data. Here are four key stockpiling models:

Server-joined capacity

System joined capacity

Capacity zone systems

Tape libraries

Server-appended capacity

Server-appended capacity is the most widely recognized kind of capacity and has maybe turned into somewhat unfashionable.

As the name suggests, the majority of the circles and gadgets used to store the information are introduced in the server itself, as opposed to in a different gadget. That makes server-appended capacity financially savvy, particularly for little and moderate size organizations (SMBs), because they won't have to purchase some other gadget or framework. This method is increasingly reasonable for little servers that help access to petition for a few PCs or clients in a little office arrange. It is additionally a dependable method to give stockpiling to an application that keeps running on a server. Be that as it may, one test organizations face with server-appended capacity is versatility, as a server can just help such a large number of hard drives. This means, on the off chance that you come up short on space and need new capacity, the main option is to utilize greater plates. Be that as it may, when your organization begins utilizing greatest circles, the movement or redesign way to a greater stockpiling system turns out to be progressively unpredictable.

Network Attached Storage (NAS)

The essential distinction among NAS and server-joined capacity is its utilization of a committed apparatus to house circle drives. NAS boxes, as they are known, associated with a system and can be gotten to by numerous customer gadgets, for example, PCs or servers. These containers are presently accessible in different sizes extending from single drive units costing a few hundred dollars each, to million-dollar frameworks each pressed with many plates. NAS became a force to be reckoned with in the late 1990s as an approach to enable servers to run applications quicker, easing the server from conveying information documents to clients. This type of capacity design additionally enables organizations to keep documents and information they need now and again in a committed machine. NAS is likewise well known for its capacity to hold different circles, which enables the reflecting of information to guarantee unwavering quality and information security. NAS machines have multiplied into numerous expert structures. In smaller-scale or independent ventures, NAS units are regularly utilized as a substitute for a server. In enormous organizations, master NAS gadgets speed access to information, for example, databases or email chronicles. Bigger organizations use NAS as a spot to store information they use oftentimes, as opposed to producing system traffic that courses through other capacity machines, for example, stockpiling region systems.

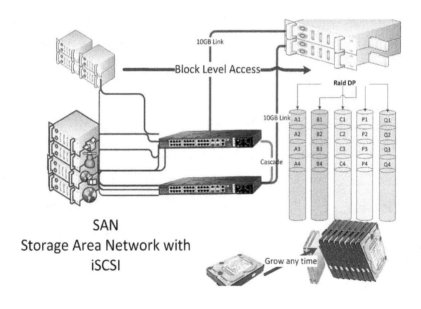

Storage Area Network (SAN)

The present most progressive stockpiling choice is a capacity region to arrange (SAN). These capacity systems can include at least one stockpiling gadgets, however, are seen by applications and servers as a solitary wellspring of information. This is significant for clients who need a ton of capacity limit because by joining gadgets into a solitary legitimate substance, SAN bolsters the utilization of various gadgets with various abilities to store information of various significance. These capacity systems are likewise incredible because they enable organizations to more readily control their capacity costs by mixing various kinds of capacity equipment in a solitary coherent unit. Records that are utilized each day, for instance, can be put away on quick, costly plates so clients can get to them instantly. More seasoned information that is just gotten to once a month can be moved off to more established, increasingly slow capacity gadgets. Access to the information here is slower however since the documents are utilized less now and again, client desires can be better overseen. Since these capacity choices live in a solitary SAN, which the working framework oversees as one single unit, organizations can blend and match stockpiling to accomplish higher execution and value proportion. One significant component organizations must remember is that, with SAN, they should send and deal with a system to associate their capacity gadgets. This system can be executed dependent on Fiber Channel, a convention that is full-grown and broadly conveyed and gives quicker, progressively complex access to information. Be that as it may, this type of system is more costly to obtain and work than an Ethernet arrange. Fiber Channel is all the more expensive because such arrange frameworks sell at much lower volumes than Ethernet. All things considered, there are less prepared specialists fit for working a fiber channel system and this drives up work and in general costs for such organizes. An opponent Ethernet-based standard Internet SCSI (iSCSI), has since developed, giving paces moving toward 10Gbps, contrasted with Fiber Channel's 8Gbps. Whichever stage an association picks, it ought to recall that speed is significant if its representatives frequently get to bigger documents - an undertaking for which SANs are perfect on account of their entrance speed capacities.

Tape and tape libraries

Any of the capacity advancements referenced above are more than equipped for making reinforcements for an organization's information documents. All can be conveyed with Redundant Arrays of Inexpensive Disks (RAID), an innovation that permits the coordinated utilization of at least two hard drives so organizations can achieve better repetition, and henceforth, more prominent execution and information unwavering quality. Be that as it may, long haul information stockpiling on the circle is not a typical practice since plate stockpiling is still nearly more costly than tape. Moreover, plates work inside servers so NASs or SANs expend control at whatever point they are being used, and this can be an exorbitant domain for

SMBs to keep up - just as a situation that isn't eco-accommodating for its high vitality utilization. Another contention against the utilization of plate as reinforcement is its cumbersomeness. The tape is, in this way, regularly pushed as the most ideal approach to store reinforcements and long haul documents. Tapes are commonly less expensive than plate since they can be put away on the rack, rather than inside a circle exhibit, and devour less power. Tape additionally has the benefit of being inactive when not being used, which means they break less regularly than plates. An amazing cluster of tape drives is accessible in the market today, going to top-end tape library frameworks that mechanize the capacity and recovery of tapes, making it simple to get to the tape- - and information - organizations need to recover. Getting to information from tape, notwithstanding, accepts somewhat longer as organizations still need to distinguish and find the suitable piece of tape to recover specific information they need. Circles, on the other hand, take into account the recovery of any record or information inside minutes.

The staff in Internet technology send machines that are a virtual great rate, they unavoidably arrive at the presentation furthest reaches of the turning plates, surpassing most extreme stockpiling IOPS before arriving at the greatest limit. Accordingly, there is a lot of unutilized limits. There are four principal segments of virtualization;

The central processing unit (CPU)

Memory

Circle stockpiling

System

The work of the CPU power is that it keeps on expanding as per Moore's Law, multiplying roughly like clockwork by giving a consistently expanding number of handling centers and clock speeds. We likewise observe memory sizes expanding quickly attributable to ease RAM modules and quicker network, for example, here are 10 gigabit Ethernet, fiber channel 8gb, and Infiniband 40gb.

The majority the said permits, the VMs that are to be sent at expanded degrees of execution. Whilst we take a gander at plate innovation, in any case, great turning circles stay restricted by their involuntary parts, compelling IOPS in this manner the quantity of VMs they can bolster. Even though the SSD innovation may change this association, it is probably not going to move toward becoming standard as essential stockpiling for quite a long while as a result of cost/limit imperatives and unwavering quality concerns. Along these lines, as the IT business' hunger for more noteworthy quantities of VMs develops, it puts a huge weight on the capacity framework an issue that must be tended to by progressively effective plan.

At what time did capacity become so basic?

When you make servers virtual clients, they can separate them in between equipment quickly and with no vacation, while excluding the seen machine for them to be viewed as little than the CPU with the memory and I/O. On the other hand, in a VM domain, the capacity framework develops insignificance, as it turns into the supporting of the whole foundation. In a virtualized domain the customary framework circles are provisioned from the focal stockpiling, including load as well as adding to the randomized information access design the same number of virtual servers simultaneously fight for plate assets.

Think about this model: Admin A requires to solidify and make virtual the framework Let us say they own 25 window servers, MS Exchange, Linux servers, two little SQL databases, ERP framework and also client host indexes. The overseer in this situation will frequently put resources into a few new servers which have radically expanded CPU centers and give memory required yet may disregard to measure the capacity framework appropriately. The issues begin here because numerous elements, including limit, sorts of the RAID levels, and that of drivers as well as irregular execution of I/O should be taken into consideration.

Execution versus limit

Within the exemplary plate coerce showcase, huge limit increments happen at regular intervals. Be that as it may, we don't see a critical increment in turning plate execution. Execution outcomes continue as before. Back then, it might have displayed a test, as circle limit stayed down in that many SAN arrangements involve of 50+ plates to give any helpful limit. This numerous plates gave a lot of IOPS for every GB of limit. In the present innovation atmosphere, a pervasiveness of savvy SATA drives could give a similar limit of a fifth or sixth of the required number of plates contrasted and also SAS drives. The quantity of IOPS diminishes with the utilization of SATA drives which whenever utilized in a requesting irregular I/O condition like an exceptionally value-based file or enormous servers that are virtual, the SATA circles and their IOPS ability will block well prior to as far as possible is come to, except if they are led with strong condition reserve, where it can expand the framework's arbitrary in I/O execution by many times. It's additionally of value taking a gander with the rough manageable cost purposes of various circle innovations: During the IOPS run of 100-3000 run, the SATA drives give a very financially savvy stage, with estimating as a rule given in terms of per GB dollars. The SAS are generally in automatic innovation, as arriving at this SATA exhibition needs countless shafts or measure of SSD reserving. Elite plates are normally estimated up cost for each GB. In the 10,000+ IOPS run, SSD starts to bode well, as just a small amount of clients general stockpiling requires such degrees of execution. Be that as it may, the best utilization of blaze is as a reserve.

The I/O data Patterns

The example where the request or the host' server peruses information can essentially influence the presentation of the capacity framework. Information examples are normally alluded to as either arbitrary or successive. An irregular information example suggests that the information is composed of arbitrary regions of the circle platter. With these, there are two fundamental impacts on a RAID exhibition framework. First, there is decreasing of the controller reserve viability, with which depends on examples to 'surmise' which information squares will be perused or composed straightaway. In irregular information design, this is beyond the realm of imagination, since an arbitrary grouping of occasions can never be 'speculated' and, accordingly, stored, however, 'hot information' tends to float into the reserve. The second pivotal impact of arbitrary examples is an expanded number of 'looks for': the time when a plate head must move to the following mentioned information square. If this square is haphazardly set, the plate's head and implementor have to go a huge separation in search of the square for every compose. In the circumstance includes overhead that is huge and also lessens execution. For instance, SATA drives, which utilize bigger circle platters, endure under arbitrary outstanding tasks at hand, as they just turn at 7200rpm and also have an extended look for and entry times. There are more qualified SAS drives just for the reason that they have platters that are littler and turn at the rate of 15000rpm, which also they look for in a moment of a fraction of the selected time (3.3ms by and large). Due to lack of moving parts, SSD is an option in the outrageous elite apps which makes it non-existent to look for times.

With an irregular remaining task at hand, turn rate and right to use time are usually vital to turning circle execution. The quicker a circle turns, then the IOPS will be more. On the other hand, one of the structures is successive information and consistency: an instance, information reinforcement as well as video gushing. Within these apps, then the records are normally enormous and also kept in touch with the plate in nonstop squares and areas. Given this, the RAID controller and plates can all the more effectively 'surmise' and additionally store the looming information squares to expand execution. Moreover, there is no need to move the header and actuator arm of the plate in an incredible separation to look for the mentioned square. Such successive apps are generally planned when within MBs. This structure is infrequently constrained by plate speed and all the more ordinarily restricted by the controller and interconnect. Along these lines, in a capacity structure for consecutive applications, such as SATA, SSD and SAS circles give fundamentally the same as execution levels. The fast decide guideline is that consecutive examples are those with huge or gushing records and are most appropriate to SATA drives. Arbitrary remaining tasks at hand are commonly those with little documents or capacity demands that have no steady structure (virtual servers, virtual work areas, value-based databases, etc) and are most appropriate to SSD or conceivably SAS.

The RAID Effect

The comprehending of information examples, as well as plate kinds, are urgent during planning to stockpile for explicit applications, however, RAID level/type should likewise be considered. The capacity idea of 'equality punishment' alludes to the exhibition cost or effect of securing information through RAID. This punishment is only available on composes, therefore it is essential to recognize whether the earth is composed or perused escalated. These are the RAID insurance equality punishments: Peruses In light of these compose overhead costs, think about the accompanying: SSD drives are intended for irregular outstanding tasks at hand, so they ought to ordinarily be arranged as RAID1+0 to augment execution (except if a domain is 100% perused). SAS drives are additionally gone for execution. Along these lines, there ought to be the utilization of RAID 1+0 or RAID 5.

Enormous limits of SATA drives are usually gone for limit with throughput ought to be arranged as RAID6. RAID6 likewise gives extra security and true serenity during remakes for reinforcement apps where SATA the drives are liked. There can be viewing of RAID 5 when utilizing 2TB drives or littler. RAID1+0 can likewise be believed in exceptionally top-ranked virtual frameworks of about 2000 machines.

Structuring the capacity framework

The good way of structuring a productive stockpiling arrangement is getting application and condition necessities. Building up the information to plan the correct engineering can emerge out of specialized gatherings and talks, remote examination, on-location expert administrations and contemplating apps good practice IOPS control necessities for the SQL, VMware View, Exchange, or different apps explicit to nature. For each situation, the fundamental objective is to decide whether the earth/application is consecutive or arbitrary. Next, find the necessities for limit, IOPS, and MBs. However, there could be necessities used for capacity capacities, for example, depictions and duplication. In any case, the information full detail is inaccessible, basically with knowledge in the working framework and apps will provide you with guidance within the structure. The I/O stat can be used for requesting servers within the client condition can be checked utilizing (Unix) or Perfmon (Windows). At the point when utilized accurately, these implicit instruments can give every one of the information required. Another alternative is to utilize outsider observing applications, for example, VMware Capacity Planner. Such applications will accumulate nitty-gritty execution data and produce stockpiling reports. At last, you may assemble execution measurements from your current stockpiling framework. This information offers a beginning stage for planning the capacity arrangement. In an irregular condition, you will require to adjust and limit IOPS. In a successive domain, the structure will concentrate on limit and throughput or MB/s. Significantly, consecutive stockpiling frameworks are a lot simpler to design, as the MB/s appraisals quite often surpass the prerequisites.

Importance of Data storage

In the beginning, it is necessary to discuss the significance of data. The sheer volume of information combined with the improved investigation abilities accessible today implies that organizations currently can show signs of improvement comprehension of how their clients act in the at various times just as potentially what's to come. This veritable abundance of information can be mined and controlled into noteworthy data that can help take care of key business issues, sell more items or administrations, and everything in the middle. Information examination has turned into a significant focused separation from which most any business can profit.

Importance of storage

Because of its supreme volume, how and where organizations store this consistently developing pool of information has turned out to could easily compare to ever. The IT foundation must most likely scale with development and keep on giving reliable degrees of execution.

However, the truth for some is that server farms are coming up short on space in offices with premium expense per square foot. Moreover, inheritance circle based capacity can't convey reliably against new execution necessities. Putting away information isn't just about how and where, yet also, the speed wherein it very well may be gotten to, controlled, and introduced. For instance, getting to information in 5-10 ms is simply unreasonably delayed for an information-driven business that is reacting progressively to worldwide business openings on a 24×7 premise.

Because of its characteristic innovative favorable circumstances, an flash storage arrangement can illuminate a considerable lot of the present information development and availability issues in a denser, progressively productive, and littler structure factor. This empowers a higher level of capacity combination inside each 42U rack, sparing enormously on server farm space. This expanded rack thickness is balanced by power and cooling investment funds of up to 80% along these lines empowering server farms to remain inside their capacity envelope for each rack on the floor. Also, with progression in glimmer innovation, the descending value bend implies that every single blaze arrangement would now be able to be procured at a similar expense as customary endeavor plate stockpiling.

Simultaneously, streak based capacity conveys higher I/O execution, which is by and large 10-15x quicker than heritage stockpiling. Blaze can recover information in microseconds, as opposed to milliseconds, which is fundamental for constant or other execution delicate remaining burdens. Along these lines, glimmer conveys higher thickness and execution at the practically identical expense.

Virtualization Architecture

The term virtualization extensively depicts the detachment of an asset or solicitation for an administration which comes from the hidden seen conveyance of the administration. Using virtual memory as an example, PC programming accesses large memory chunk than what is initially introduced, using the foundation exchanging of information to circle stockpiling. Additionally, the virtualization strategies can be connected to other layers of the foundation levels which also include systems, stockpiling, PC or server equipment, working frameworks, and apps. The sending of the virtual foundation is non-problematic since the client encounters are to a great extent unaltered. In any case, the virtual framework gives heads the upside of overseeing pooled assets over the enterprise, enabling IT supervisors to be increasingly receptive to diverse authoritative needs and also all the more likely influence foundation speculations. Utilizing virtual framework arrangements, for example, those from VM ware, venture IT supervisors should be able to attend to difficulties that comprise: Consolidation of server, and also sprawl containment using framework sending which act as virtual machines. This is VMs that can securely run and go straightforwardly crosswise over communal equipment, as well as increment server usage speed which ranges 5-15 to 60-80.

The test and development optimization quickly provides test and improvement servers which include reusing of pre-arranged frameworks and also upgrading designer joint effort and standardizing advancement situations. Advancement of Business- Decreasing of the expense and intricacy of business progression which includes high accessibility and calamity recuperation arrangements) by typifying whole frameworks into single documents that can be imitated and reestablished on any objective server, accordingly limiting vacation. Undertaking the work stations and Desktop Securing unmanaged PCs, where there is no trading off end client self-rule by leveling a safety approach in programming around work area virtual machines.

Virtualization Approaches

Whilst virtualization is a piece of the IT scene for quite a long time, it is as of late that the advantages virtualization were conveyed by VMware to the industry value set stages, which currently structure most of the work area, workstation as well as shipment of servers. A key virtualization advantage involves the capacity to run different working frameworks on a solitary physical framework and offer the fundamental equipment assets known as parceling. Hypervisors can be intended to stay firmly combined with the working frameworks or else rationalist to working frameworks. Additionally, the last approach furnishes clients with the capacity to execute a nonpartisan of an OS administration worldview, consequently giving further legitimization of the server farm. The parceling of the level of application is yet another methodology, where numerous apps share a solitary working framework, yet this offers less seclusion (and higher hazard) than equipment or programming dividing, and constrained help for heritage applications or heterogeneous conditions. Be that as it may, different dividing methods can be joined, but with expanded unpredictability. Thus, virtualization is a wide IT activity, of which apportioning is only one aspect.

Different advantages incorporate the detachment of the virtual machines and the equipment autonomy that outcomes from the virtualization procedure. One outstanding advantage is the compactness of the virtual machines which can also be shifted and copied to any acceptable standard in the industry equipment stage, paying little heed to the make or model. In this way, virtualization encourages versatile IT asset the board and more noteworthy responsiveness to changing business conditions. To give favorable circumstances past parceling, a few framework assets have to be virtualized and overseen. This includes the Central processing units, I/O and principle memory notwithstanding having a between segment asset the board capacity. While parceling is a helpful capacity for IT associations, a genuine virtual framework conveys business worth well that has past that.

The Virtualization for the Server Consolidation and Containment- Virtual framework activities regularly leap from server farm server union tasks, which spotlight on decreasing existing foundation "box tally", resigning more seasoned equipment expanding inheritance apps. The solidification of server advantages come from a decrease in the general number of frameworks and related repeating costs which involve control, rack space, cooling and so forth. Whilst server solidification tends to the decrease of the present foundation, server control takes a progressively key view, server regulation takes an increasingly vital view, server containment leading to an objective of framework unification. Server containment utilizes a gradual way to deal with outstanding burden virtualization, where new ventures are provided with machines that are virtual instead of the servers that are physical, in this manner conceding equipment buys. It's essential to take note of that solidification nor repression ought to be seen as an independent implementation. Either way, the most noteworthy advantages come about because of embracing an all-out expense of-proprietorship (TCO) point of view, with an attention on the progressing, repeating backing and the board costs, notwithstanding onetime, direct costs. Server farm conditions are winding up increasingly mind-boggling and heterogeneous, with correspondingly higher administration costs. Virtual foundation empowers increasingly powerful improvement of IT assets, through the institutionalization of server farm components that should be overseen. Apportioning alone does not convey server union or control, and thus solidification does not liken to full virtual foundation the board. Past segmenting and fundamental part level asset the board, a center arrangement of frameworks the board abilities are required to adequately actualize sensible server farm solutions. These the executive's capacities should incorporate exhaustive framework asset observing (of measurements, for example, CPU action, circle get to, memory usage and system data transmission), mechanized provisioning, high accessibility and the remaining task at hand relocation support. These administration capacities should incorporate extensive framework asset observing (of measurements, for example, CPU action, circle get to, memory use and system data transfer capacity), mechanized provisioning, high accessibility, and outstanding burden relocation hold.

The complementing of virtualization New Generation Hardware Extensive 'scale-out' and multi-level application models are ending up progressively normal, and the appropriation of littler structure factor edge servers is developing significantly. Since the change to edge designs is commonly determined by a longing for a physical combination of IT assets, virtualization is a perfect supplement for cutting edge servers, conveying advantages, for example, asset enhancement, operational effectiveness, and quick provisioning. The most recent age of x86-based frameworks highlight processors with 64-piece augmentations supporting memories with large space. With this, there is the improvement of their ability to have huge, serious memory apps, just as permitting a lot increasingly machines that are virtual to be facilitated by a server that is physically conveyed inside a virtual system. The consistent abatement in the cost of memory costs will further quicken this pattern. In like manner, the approaching double center processor innovation altogether benefits IT associations by drastically bringing down the expenses of expanded execution. Contrasted with conventional single-center frameworks, frameworks using double center processors will be more affordable since just a large portion of the attachments numbers which are to be needed in a similar number of CPUs.

Essentially, by bringing down the multi-processor expense frameworks, double center innovation will quicken server farm union and virtual foundation ventures. Past these upgrades, the VMware is additionally toiling intimately to guarantee that the technology of the processor of intel and AMD highlights virtual framework to the furthest reaches. Specifically, the new virtualization equipment assists in supporting Intel and AMD and will empower powerful CPU virtualization usefulness. In such equipment virtualization backing does not supplant virtual foundation, however, enables it to run all the more productively.

Paravirtualization - Even though virtualization is quickly getting to be standard technology, the idea has pulled in an enormous measure of premium, and upgrades keep on being explored. One of these is paravirtualization, whereby working framework similarity is exchanged against execution for specific CPU-bound apps which run on frameworks even without virtualization equipment help. There possible performance in the para-virtualized model and gives advantages when a visitor working framework concerned that it is working inside a virtualized domain, and also adjusted to misuse this. One potential drawback of this methodology is that such adjusted visitors can't ever be relocated back to keep running on physical equipment.

Before actualizing virtualized frameworks, you have to decide the sort of virtualization engineering to use in your datacenter. There are two noteworthy sorts of virtualization engineering: facilitated and exposed metal.

Facilitated Architecture

In facilitated design, a working framework (OS) is introduced on the equipment first. Next programming, a hypervisor or virtual machine screen is introduced. This product is utilized to introduce different visitor activity frameworks, or virtual machines (VMs), on the equipment. Applications are then introduced and kept running on the virtual machines similarly as on a physical machine. Facilitated virtualization engineering is increasingly helpful for programming advancement, running inheritance applications, and supporting distinctive working frameworks.

Exposed metal Architecture

With the exposed metal design, the hypervisor is introduced straightforwardly on the equipment instead of over a hidden working framework. VMs and their applications are introduced on the hypervisor similarly as with facilitated design. Applications that give constant access or information preparing advantage from uncovered metal virtualization desi

Chapter 3: Transmission control protocol (TCP) and IMPLEMENTATION

The Transmission Control Protocol (TCP). It's the system model utilized during the present web engineering also. Conventions are a set of principles which administer each conceivable correspondence over a system. These conventions portray the development of information in between the foundation as well as the goal. They additionally offer straight forward giving the names and also tending to plans.

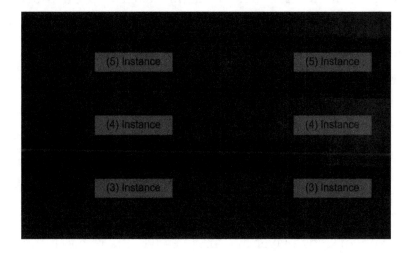

Overview of TCP

The department of defense project research agency(ARPA, which changed to DARPA) created Transmission Control Protocol and Internet Protocol as a piece of an examination venture of system interconnection to interface remote machines. The highlights were outstanding during the exploration, which prompted making the TCP/IP reference model were:

• Sustaining adaptable engineering. Additional more machines in the system were simple.

• The system was powerful, and the associations stayed unblemished until the host and goal mechanisms were working.

The general thought was to enable each app on the PC to spread information on another PC. Various levels of TCP/IP reference Model Beneath have talked about the 4 layers that structure the TCP/IP referal model:

Hardware layer

The Hardware layer is in charge of precisely that equipment. This incorporates links, the repeaters and interface documents. It acknowledges the information go to it through the Network edge layer and prefixes what is referred to as the Preamble, where there is a notable succession bit utilized for management. And when the work is complete, it creates a sign to give to the electronic media link as a rule. The Hardware layer additionally forces the most extreme exchange component utilized by the level of the internet to guarantee the hardware doesn't get frames3 that are excessively enormous or excessively little. There involve two equipment gadgets in which they work at this level: This includes Repeaters and speakers

A repeater is a gadget with various ports normally that is equipped for accepting sign, sifting through clamor (marvels not identified with the current correspondence), and rehashing the sign to each port aside from the entrance (approaching) port. Speakers play out a similar

assignment, then again, actually they don't channel clamor. Thusly, repeaters are utilized in electrical correspondences conditions and intensifiers are utilized in light-based interchanges situations. These gadgets are frequently called center points or concentrators.

The Network Interface Layer

The addition of drivers of the gadgets is regarded to the network Interface layer. It has to set up the information from the internet level to the flagging. This is done by prefixing the header, affixing the datagram by adding CRC and also spreading this data into the gadget interface, motioning which is termed casing. Specifically, this level comprehends seen locations regularly termed to as the Media Access Control [MAC] addresses. During the utilization of Ethernet, it is frequently termed as an Ethernet address. The physical locations are neighborhood and just should be remarkable inside the nearby arrange. There are 48 chipsets of the Ethernet addresses for all time composed into readable programs. This layer involves the goal and the foundation location in the header in epitome. Thus, at this level deep capsulation, beginning choices are made about whether to keep preparing an approaching edge up the stack. A switch is the one gadget that is well related to this layer. The Switches look particularly like repeaters, a bit of equipment within any event two system ports, yet are shrewd than the repeaters. Since they work at the Network Interface layer, they can settle on choices dependent on physical locations. Switches are here and there called center points or scaffolds or layer two switches.

The Internet Layer

The Internet layer is in charge of an assortment of undertakings. To achieve these assignments it utilizes three head conventions. The IP is in charge of directing and discontinuity. The ICMP creates blunder messages, helps directing through redirection, may execute simple stream control, bolsters the ping order, underpins switch disclosure, and may produce time stamp and net cover inquiries and reactions. The IGMP underpins the Internet Layer multicasting. Every one of the professional tools has double accessible forms four and 6. The gadget that works at this level is a switch. Switches are hubs that actualize the knowledge of the net level conventions and forward information grams to the fitting systems or sub-systems dependent on IP addresses and the directing calculation. Switches are in some cases called layer 3 switches. Lamentably, switches are additionally in some cases called center points. The Internet level delivers or peruses the Internet level header. It involves great deal of data and, specifically, incorporates the host and goal of the IP address related to the bundle. There involves two renditions of the protocols in this level: adaptation four and variant six. These are worldwide locations, implying that all hubs all through an accumulation of systems that are interconnected (web) must be exceptionally recognized by this location. Information is gone through such a web by the way toward directing. Steering is carried out by analyzing a segment of an IP address to decide to which system the information should be sent (adequately the reason for the directing calculation). Linux frameworks can go about as switches.

The Transport level

It is responsible for the start to finish

stream of information. It chooses if information transmission ought to be in a parallel way or single way.

1. Functions, for example, multiplexing, sectioning or parting on the information is finished by vehicle layer.

2. The applications can peruse and keep in touch with the vehicle layer.

3. Transport level positions in header data to the information.

4. Transport level splits the information hooked on little elements with the goal that they are

taken care of all the more productively by the system layer.

5. The Transport layer additionally masterminds the parcels to be sent, in succession.

The Application Level

Every application lives in the Application layer. The applications are accountable for being aware of the information group just as translating the information. The sample apps incorporate the Dynamic host configuration protocol (DHCP), The network file system (NFS), Domain Name Service (DNS), Electronic email, Samba, the document move convention(FTP), and also telnet utility. One of the gadgets that work on this level is the entryway. Tragically, the passage is a term, to some degree like center, that is utilized from multiple points of view. We, for the most part, characterize it to mean a connection among unmistakable and additionally extraordinary PC systems. Frequently, it is used to allude to a framework that is equipped for changing over starting with one system protocol stack then onto the next, for example, a framework which is linked into TCP/IP and also net ware. The door is frequently utilized to allude to a framework that links an inner web work and an outer system, for example, the Internet. Different employments of the term portal are portrayed as they emerge.

The TCP/IP model Benefits

1. It worked autonomously.

2. It is adaptable.

3.Client/server The design of client/server.

4. It holds up various steering conventions.

5. Can be utilized to build up an association between two PCs.

Disadvantages of TCP/IP

1. Usually, the vehicle level doesn't ensure conveyance of bundles.

2. this model cannot be utilized in another app.

3. Substituting the convention isn't simple.

4. It has not isolated its administrations, interfaces, and convention

Since the ascent of TCP Reno, a few TCP options in contrast to Reno have been built up; every endeavor to administer the apparent Reno inadequacy. Whilst a large number is quite certain endeavors in dealing with the high bandwidth issue which was considered the High Bandwidth TCP issues, a number of them concentrate principally or totally on the shortfalls of TCP Reno. Such a problem is TCP Reno's "avarice" regarding line usage; another is the lossy interface issue experienced by, state, Wi-Fi clients. As a rule, the usage of TCP reacts to clog during the bluff which can react to bundle misfortunes or else react when there is a blockage, it can distinguish the expansion in RTT related with the filling of the line. These methodologies are some of the time alluded to as misfortune with the basis of the delay based separately; the last term as a result of the ascent in the RTT. The TCP implementers can have changed in both the misfortune reaction the multiple reductions of the TCP Reno and furthermore how TCP expands its CWND in the non-attendance of misfortune. There involves an assortment of the high value of choices accessible. The idea of observing the RTT maintain a strategic distance from blockage at the knee was first presented in TCP. The one outstanding element of the TCP Vegas is, without rivalry, the line can never fill, and accordingly there could be no congestive misfortunes. The TCP saw tooth, at the end of the day, isn't unavoidable. At the point when misfortunes do happen, the greater part of the components explored here keep on utilizing the TCP New Reno recuperation methodology. As the greater part of executions here are moderate, later senders can, by and large, be expecting the end will bolster SACK TCP, which permits increasingly fast recuperation from different misfortunes.

High bandwidth

One objective of the TCP usage that endeavors in attaching the High transmission capacity issue are to be unreasonable in the TCP Reno: general-purpose involves permitting CWND in expanding further forcefully than what is allowed by Reno. Past that, we can survey what another thing the TCP rendition ought to do. The first one is the regressive similarity imperative: A new TCP is needed to display sensible decency with TCP Reno at lower data transfer capacity defer items. Specifically, it ought to not have a fundamentally lesser cwnd than what a contending TCP Reno would. Yet, also, it ought not to take data transfer capacity from a TCP Reno association unreasonably. The remark above on the shamefulness to Reno, in any case, the original TCP, when contending with the TCP Reno, can shift the Reno association with a similar transmission capacity it would have on the off chance that it was rivaling another Reno association. This is conceivable because at higher bandwidth-delay items TCP Reno does not effectively utilize the accessible transmission capacity; the new TCP ought to the degree conceivable confine itself to devouring this already inaccessible data transfer capacity as opposed to eating essentially into the data transmission of a contending TCP Reno association. There is additionally the self decency issue: different associations utilizing the new TCP ought to get comparable data transfer capacity assignments, at any rate with comparable RTTs. For disparate RTTs, the data transfer capacity extents ought to in a perfect world be no more terrible than they would be under TCP Reno. In a perfect world, we additionally need the moderately fast assembly to decency; reasonableness is something of an empty guarantee if just associations moving at the rate of a gigabit will profit by it. In the case of the TCP Reno, two associations divide the distinction in their separate funds at each mutual misfortune occasion; more slow intermingling is conceivable. It is more enthusiastically to seek after decency between contending new executions. In any case, at any rate, on the off chance that new executions tcp1 and tcp2 are contending, at that point neither ought to get not as much as TCP Reno would get. Some new TCPs utilize cautious RTT estimations, and, as we will see beneath, such estimations are liable to a significant level of commotion. Any new TCP execution ought to be sensibly strong even with mistakes in RTT estimation; an unassuming or transient estimation blunder ought not to cause the convention to carry on seriously, with either heading of less cwnd. At long last, another TCP ought to in a perfect world attempt to keep away from groups of different misfortunes at every misfortune occasion. Such various misfortunes, for instance, are an issue for TCP New Reno with no SACK: normally, one RTT is needed to every bundle that is lost. Indeed, when having SACK, numerous misfortunes confound recuperation. However, on the off chance that another TCP increases cwnd by a sum N>1 on each RTT, at that point, the system roof can be passed because the system has the ability while making N group misfortunes sensibly prone to happen. The misfortunes could be circulated among all associations, not simply the new-TCP one. All TCPs tending to the high-transmission capacity issue will require a cwnd increase N that is genuinely enormous, probably a portion of the time, clearly clashing with this no- various misfortune perfect. One stunt is to decrease N when bundle misfortune has all the earmarks of being approaching. There are instruments of TCP Illinois and cubic which are set up to decrease various misfortunes.

Round Trip Time (RTT)

The accurate exhibition of a portion of the quicker TCPs we consider so far as that is concerned, the careful TCP Reno presentation is impacted through the RTT. This usually influences singular TCP execution and furthermore rivalry between various TCPs. For mention, here is a couple of average RTTs from Chicago to different spots:

• Southeast Asia 100-200 ms

• The United states west coast 50-100ms

• The Europe 100-50ms

We begin with the High-speed TCP, which is a pioneer and moderately straightforward endeavor to deal with the high transfer speed TCP issue. The activity that follows is the TCP Vegas, TCP Westwood, TCP Fast, and compound TCP gathering. These all include supposed postponement based blockage control, in which the sender cautiously screens the RTT for the moment builds that sign lining. TCP Vegas, which dates from 1995, is the most punctual TCP here and in certainty originates before across the board acknowledgment of the high-transmission capacity TCP issue. Its objective at that point and now was to demonstrate that one could fabricate a TCP that, without rivalry, could move subjectively long surges of information without any misfortunes

and with complete block interface usage. The next gathering, comprising of TCP Veno, TCP Hybla and DCTCP, speak to specific reason TCPs. While TCP Veno might be a sensible high- data transfer capacity TCP up-and-comer, it's essential objective is to get better TCP execution on bad connections, for example, the Wifi. The satellite internet uses TCP Hybla with extended RTTs whereas DCTCP is used for inside associations inside an information center which has RTTs that are short. The final set of three speaks to more up to date, no delay endeavors for tackling the elevated transfer speed TCP issue:

HTCP, TCP Cubic, and TCP BBR. TCP Cubic has turned into the TCP on Linux default.

High-Speed TCP

The proposed repair for TCP high transfer speed issue is the high-speed TCP, which is reported by Floyd in 2003. The High-speed TCP is usually here and there termed HS-TCP, however, there is utilization the more drawn out name her to stay away from perplexity with the disconnected H-TCP, beneath. High-speed TCP alters the added substance increment and multiplier decline structures in order, for bigger estimations of cwnd, the pace increment among misfortunes is a lot quicker, therefore the cwnd decline at misfortune occasions is a lot littler. This permits effective utilization of all the accessible transfer speed for enormous delays in the band with items. Consequently, when cwnd is in the variety where TCP Reno functions admirably, TCP throughput High speed is just unassumingly bigger than the TCP Reno's, therefore both contend moderately decently. The limit for High-speed TCP separating from the TCP Reno includes a misfortune rate under 10–3, which for TCP Reno happens when cwnd = 38. Past that point, High-speed TCP step by step expands and diminishes. The general impact is to beat TCP Reno by a factor N = N(cwnd) as per the table beneath.

TCP VEGAS

The Vegas was presented in BP 95. It is the basic TCP adaptation that is we believed to be from the past century. The objective was not meant to legitimately to deal with the high transmission capacity issue, yet rather to improve TCP throughput by and large; surely, in 1995 the high data transfer capacity issue had no focus on pragmatic alarm. Eager TCP Vegas objective is basically to kill many misfortunes and also to attempt to store the blockage connect fully used consistently. Review from the TCP indicates that, with an enormous line, the normal bottleneck interface usage for the TCP Reno usually sums to less with up to 75%. The TCP Vegas accomplishes the development while perceiving TCP blockage at the center wherever the bottleneck connection has turned out to be soaked and additional cwnd expands outcome in RTT increments. A TCP Vegas propeller unaided rivalry just joined with the rest of TCP Vegas associations will only here and there if at any point approach the "precipice" where parcel misfortunes happen. To achieve this, no uncommon switch participation or significantly recipient collaboration – is essential. Rather, the sender utilizes cautious checking of the RTT to monitor the quantity of "additional bundles" (ie parcels sitting in lines) it has infused into the system. Without rivalry, the RTT will stay consistent, equivalent to no-load of RTT, in anticipation of cwnd when it expands to the moment that the bottleneck connection has turned out to be soaked and the line starts to fill. By checking the data transfer capacity too, a transmitter can decide on the genuine bundle's numbers in the bottleneck line, as transmission capacity. TCP Vegas utilizes this data to endeavor in keeping up consistently a little yet an optimistic number of parcels in the bottleneck line. The technique on TCP Vegas is presently frequently alluded to as postponement supported clog control, instead of TCP Reno's misfortune based blockage control. TCP Reno's occasional misfortunes pursued by the dividing of cwnd is the thing that prompts the "TCP sawtooth"; TCP Vegas, be that as it may, has no saw tooth. A TCP sender can promptly gauge the throughput. One of the easiest estimations is cwnd/RTT as in RTT Calculations; this adds up to averaging throughput over a whole RTT. Give us a chance to signify this transmission capacity gauge by BWE; until further notice, we will acknowledge BWE as precise. TCP Vegas gauges the no-load RTT using the base RTT experienced in the period of the association. Among the "perfect" cwnd that just soaks the bottleneck connection is BWE_RTT load. Note that BWE will be considerably more unpredictable than RTTmin; the last will commonly arrive at its last esteem right off the bat in the association, while BWE will vary here and there with clog (which will likewise follow up on RTT, yet by expanding it

Chapter 4: Planning a Network

Organization set up

The business client of information correspondences frequently applies the specialized material in this book to the arranging and structure of an information interchanges framework, or the activity and the board of the example of the framework. As a focus in this section, there is the bargain with arranging as well as the plan of information correspondence frameworks. First, we concentrate on the huge issues involving how the hierarchical technique, traditions, and approaches influence the arrangement and structuring of information correspondence frameworks. Next, we take a gander at orderly methods for arranging and plan. Arranging and structuring of information correspondence systems are massively complex. In the first place, we usually confine to arranging as well as de-marking medium-size systems.

With these, they are most habitually claimed by the firms due to their very personal utilization; which is, private systems. This prohibits the enormous web works, particularly the open systems actualized by correspondence administration sellers with an example of the phone organizations, and also the huge Internet specialist organizations. Finally, we don't consider systems that are little to the point that they can be purchased out of the container" and for which the arranging, plan, and execution can all be carried out by not very many individuals, maybe just one. We center essentially around the network planning and plan issues of client associations with noteworthy coordination issues; this normally implies wide zone systems. Before an information correspondences venture even gets to the formal plausibility thinks about that piece of the improvement philosophy that is advocated in this segment, it is important to list down, subjective assessment of accepted information interchanges arrangement. In that assessment, there is no need for consuming a lot of time or assets and this can lead to an outcome of hasty endeavors in the beginning. With this assessment, there needs to begin from an unmistakable comprehending of the systems approaches, and also the association tradition which will be using the framework. One's business for the recommended app should likewise be comprehended.

For example, someone ought to make certain that the undertaking isn't implemented because some progressed or innovation appears to be fascinating. Also, a person should be careful and cautious in that concentrating too barely on business should not put boundaries or mislead the specialized methodology. Because information activities occur in a domain of quick mechanical progression, it is useful to intently look at innovative hazard. At long last, outside elements, for example, government strategy and guideline, the focused circumstance, and accessible technological services and items must be considered.

Strategy and Culture

Strategy and Culture In a perfect world, any information correspondences undertaking ought to be arranged with regards to an organizational data methodology and strategy. Formal and casual approaches in regards to re-appropriating, turnkey obtainment, purchasing of administrations, and in-house development are significant. Once in awhile approaches influence the utilization of open over with the private networks. The measure of the human and specialized assets in the information correspondence purpose of the association additionally emphatically influences these decisions. Building up touchy mindfulness of the hierarchical traditions getting into a task helps stay away from upcoming despondency. For instance, it is critical to be aware of the association you want on putting centrally administration range. For the most part, however not generally, the executives of an association's system which is incorporated by whether the general administration organization is concentrated. Regrettable, electronic correspondence is so omnipresent in present-day business that it is difficult to build up a by and large vital vision that is far-reaching and at the same point by point enough to be helpful. Be that as it may, an unassuming exertion can yield a procedure to guide the advancement.

PLANNING

It's essential to own up professional arranging system for the nontrivial venture. As much as there are many venture arranging techniques; nonetheless, most are comparative. Numerous organizations have their own, "favored" variants, however, the mapping from the methodology we propose here to different systems ought to be sensibly clear. In most times, contended that most ventures include changes in living frameworks, hence professional framework arranging is usually tedious and gives pitiful advantageous. The contention is regularly not true for a reason as well as the end. The exponential growth of Web-based interchanges, especially online business utilizing the new systems Internet calls and upgrade of the systems that are already there, not an evolutionary change from past systems. In any case, regardless of whether the proposed venture is a seemingly straight forward improvement to existing frameworks, an arrangement of incremental changes without a well-considered system directing the advancement outcomes organizes which is dark to the client also hard to direct. Most of the techniques comprise of various steps to be carried out in the mission improvement progression. In whatever strategy, usually, it is fundamental that at the stage finishing the executives settle on an unequivocal and composed choice whether to abort the undertaking, continue to the following stage, or return to the past stage and resolve specifically characterized issues. While planning a network, it is necessary to look at the scope and the main objectives of the project. You will frequently be given a casual portrayal of the task to reach here and there casual. A fresh, unambiguous, composed characterization is important now. This portrayal ought to outline the consequences of the kind of vital, abnormal state investigation depicted toward the start of the last segment. Most of the problems to be attended to include; the one speaking and with who? Is the expert ject intended to help interchanges in the organization, correspondences with merchants and clients, interchanges with the clients, or also a blend all? What needs to be imparted? What is involved in the business functions of the system support? What, when all is said in done named, is usually the business proportion for the task? What is the period for the proposed venture?

Feasibility study

In the feasibility analysis for an undertaking is significant due to the typically the last operation opportunity to roll out real improvements in the venture before considerable assets are expended. Now quantitative cost/advantage examinations are needed to enhance undertaking has an exclusive standard of achievement. Some portion of the possible analysis is to enhance certain that the spending limit, as well as time stipend, is adequate on behalf of the destinations that are explained the underlying procedure. The practicality analysis

94

is founded on suppositions which should be expressed, recorded as a hard copy. In the case of, during the venture, at least one of these assumptions winds up invalid, a quick evaluation of the task ought to be made to check whether modifications are expected to look after achievability. Another examination required at this point is of mechanical hazard. Picking precisely which age of technology to use is major. Lamentably, fitting innovation is a progressive objective. In many ventures, accessible innovation will look up fundamentally in the time of realization. The most prevalent pointer of the outstanding development of PC tech is Moore's law, where, in one of its signs, reveals the work of the computer chips as estimated using the quantity of the transistor pairs each 18months. Regardless, a venture, particularly a gradually creating one, will discover technology developing below its feet.

Analysis

The objective in here is to sharpen and make equally the objectives of the first step;

This starts with deciding the direct organizations to be used, for instance, voice, data, Web organizations, virtual business, and various types of blended media. To the rate possible, future organizations must be suited as well. For every organization, one must assess the recent traffic and adventure this clog into what is to come. Particularly irksome is traffic showing for new or foreseen organizations for which there is no present traffic to use as a benchmark. One of the most unreasonable traffic for such a framework is what you foreseen. Either the framework misses the mark and you get less traffic, maybe none of the framework/app success, in the case you should take quick dares to thwart being overwhelmed.

Nature of organization is likewise a critical issue in the present-day important assessment. Shifting organizations require contrasting execution guarantees. For example, video and voice require stringent deferral guarantees, while data affiliations award no data setback or degradation. In this way, traffic volumes must not only be portrayed by their sources and objectives however by their inclination of organization essentials also. The dynamic idea of the traffic in like manner offers perplexities. Traffic rates have patterns and cyclic assortments that must be considered. The pile-on most data correspondence systems create with time. Likewise, traffic levels waver when of day, weekday, and the time of the year. Gathering traffic data and lessening it to a structure that can be used in the setup is very dull and slip-up slanted. The information is consistently fragmented and regularly started from various and conflicting sources. Necessities must be proficiently addressed. Each need can be addressed as a once-over of information senders, a summary of data recipients (these two records routinely include one entry each, at the same time, for the model, multicasting applications have longer ones). For every one of these prerequisites the kind of correspondence organization voice, data, various types of sight and sound must be demonstrated. For every organization, the traffic volume is required. Normally a powerful detail of the volume is basic reflecting the step by step, consistently, month to month, and yearly traffic structures and whole deal designs. Nature of-organization essentials should be shown moreover. These fuses concede impediments (both in degree and variety), the probability of pack hardship necessities, and guaranteed point of confinement, accessibility, and immovable quality (e.g., different directing). Yet again, while we portray the strategy of social occasion essentials as being self-ruling of the arrangement, in reality, the method is iterative. For the model, the use of the area supports a couple of sorts of multicasting. At the point when these headways are joined into the structure, unexpected necessities frequently appear. Luckily, present-day mastermind the board systems and rules offer sup-port for requirements examination. For example, the Management Information Base(MIB) of the Simple Network Management Protocol (SNMP) offers much valuable pattern information for the articles in existing frameworks—has, ranges, switches, and focus focuses, similarly as transmission workplaces. RMON, a remote checking standard, permits orchestrating a wide assembling of framework watching data, particularly from Ethernet LAN divides. RMON (RFCs 2021 and 1757) makes it possible to gather programmed accounts of traffic estimations, for instance, use and clog. At long last, some overall essentials must be tended to. These consolidate insurance/security issues and framework the officials' abilities.

Black box specifications

The objective is an information/yield portrayal of the framework from the client's perspective. How does the framework look at all things considered? What do clients see? What would they be able to do? Cautious thought of human variables is basic. The results in this phase include, one might say, a concurrence with the customer system describing what the correspondence framework will achieve for them. For the legitimacy of the undertaking, it is fundamental to have objective (and in a perfect world quantitative) centers for organization execution, unwavering quality, reaction, and so on with the objective that gives support to the customers and can be looked upon. To the degree conceivable, the system should consolidate modified checking of these organization destinations measures.

Options Analysis

Now, with a better than average handle of the objectives and necessities of the undertaking, one can go to the ID and appraisal of open use activities. One way to deal with do this is to use the information so far collected and prepare a Request for Information (RFI) to send to merchants to build a general thought of the hardware, workplaces, and organizations they can give that applies to the goals and necessities. In any case, you need to efficiently accumulate data on the gadgets, transmission workplaces, programming, and organizations that may be useful. For each situation, you need to know the features, costs, financing decisions (lease, buy, etc.), advantage limit, reliability of the trader, and merchant customer support.

The network architecture

The key endeavor is to browse the options perceived in the assessment of the decision the net-working approaches to managing to be taken to support the necessities. Furthermore, the verifying framework should in like manner be recognized: what components to develop, what to buy, and what to redistribute. Standards expect a huge activity in planning correspondence systems. They normally choose whether you have the prosperity of elective shippers. So you ought to pick which standards to require in your plan. In the current state of quick inventive change and uncertain prerequisites, a basic objective is to take care of flexibility: lease, don't buy; utilize acknowledged benchmarks; don't get rushed into one merchant's things or organizations. Pick innovations and structures that scale; that is destined to be, that can be agilely adjusted to help in-wrinkling demands without requiring an extreme update.

RFP

In this level, there is a build-up of the documentation where against which purchases, execution, contracts, and other cash related obligations will be made. We ought to decide in a practically stunning focal point how the structure of the correspondence is to be executed. Emissary needs and dealers may help, yet the owner is finally careful. The customers of the framework must be recognized. The territories of the equipment must be demonstrated. The applications that will be maintained must be point by point. The utmost and execution of the systems must be estimated. Security and faithful quality necessities must be introduced. The costs of equipment, transmission, and organizations (checking support and upkeep) must be explained. Organization and cutover (progress from old to new structure), together with installment plans, must be set down. The cutover plan must make courses of action for a fall back if the new structure does not execute similarly true to form with the objective that central tasks are kept up. On the off chance that possible, the new and old systems should work in standard allele until the new structure is exhibited latency. Affirmation testing should be executed as a formal procedure to find that the improvement is finished. Game plans for a customer getting ready must be made. For systems including specific hazard or various vulnerabilities, a pilot undertaking might be called for. Backing for insurance and security must be resolved. Framework the board instruments to help the movement of the framework must be shown specifically.

Implementation

This is the certified utilization of the framework. The basic activity of the coordinator/originator is to set up an intentional overview system to audit adherence to the de-pursued setup chronicle. If there ought to emerge an event of certifiable divergences, it may be essential to cycle back to earlier walks in the improvement technique and make changes. The course of action ner/organizer, generally, expect a noteworthy activity in the affirmation testing as well, which closures this progression.

Preparing and Cutover-A detailed schedule should have been set up for customer setting up that will be finished before the cutover. In case a pilot is a bit of the improvement plan, it is consistently valuable to test the arrangement structures too. A fundamental decision here is when to empower the fall-back workplaces to be disposed of.

Evaluation

After the system has been inertia for a long time, it is basic to have a planned and formal evaluation of the structure in light of operational experience. A portion of the components that should be considered is, Did the structure achieve its operational targets? Do the customers find the system responsive and trustworthy? What was/is the budgetary show? Did the endeavor come in inside spending plan? Are the operational expenses inside the spending plan? Were the cash related points of interest of the undertaking made sense of it? How does the authentic weight on the system appear differently about the master jected loads?

Redesigning/Modifications/Replacement

In basically all cases, the evaluation step will perceive various awes, much of the time unsavory. These will normally ought to be tended to by changes following the framework. Besides, it is never too early to start envisioning the redesigning or overriding the framework. A noteworthy mistake is to see system arranging and structure as an occasion rather than a procedure. Alterations, overhauls, and substitution will occur continuously. There won't be a time when triumph can be articulated and the project declared complete.

The Model

The setup methodology starts with a model of the system, consistently numerical. The model incorporates components, goals, and arrangement goals. The maker attempts to pick regards for the elements with the goal that the prerequisites are satisfied and the objective improved. We, all things considered, acknowledge that building is given and that it is only the sizes, numbers, and territories of its components similarly as their interconnections that stay to be resolved. The model of the entire trades system is involved models of traffic and solicitation, models of correspondence workplaces, and models of the terminal and exchanging gadgets. There may be various components, yet they can be parceled into two or three classifications. There are factors that measure; (a) price and return, (b) execution and unwavering quality, and (c) traffic.

In most arrangement models, the costs are disengaged into beginning costs and repeating costs. There are various variables portraying execution. Deferral, blocking, percent package disaster, throughput limit, interim among frustrations, and accessibility are models; there are various others. These variables portray the idea of administration. Describing traffic is normally the most dreary and expensive piece of the design procedure. The principle issue is that most ideal situation, you simply acknowledge what traffic there was beforehand and not what traffic there will be over the future lifetime of the proposed system. Especially in the current state of quick mechanical change, you now and again are organizing a structure for applications that did not beforehand exist or, in case they existed, were managed as of now in such an in a general sense unprecedented route from the proposed strategy that past data is of little use. Web structures to sup-port Web traffic, intelligent media, just as electronic business are typical models. The following issue is that traffic requirements must be demonstrated for each sender of data to each recipient or social affair of beneficiaries. This ideas to climb to a combinatorial impact on the required data. For instance, on the off chance that we have 100 clients, there are 9900 potential to-from sets of clients; with 1000 clients, there are 999,000 conceivable pairs. Obviously, for real frameworks, the clients must be combined into gatherings. Be that as it may, fittingly doing this isn't inconsequential. The third trouble is managing the dynamics of traffic. Traffic levels change in arbitrary courses for the time being; frequently have daily, week after week, month to month, and yearly designs. The suitable method to manage traffic dynamics relies upon the utilization of the correspondence framework. For instance, numerous retailers make the stunning bit of their arrangements in the Christmas season, and an enormous number of their correspondences structures must assistance the extraordinary traffic during this time, which could be significantly more critical than the typical weight or the store at different occasions of years. The selection of relations as objectives or the objective is somewhat subjective. Regularly one is excited about the trade-offs between these relations. For example, in one setting you might be excited about restricting ordinary deferment of messages, con-worried by the need of a given breaking point. In various settings, you may wish to boost the farthest point given an upper bound on the typical deferral as an objective.

System Design Tools and Algorithms

Network configuration devices **are** frameworks worked **around suites of** structure calculations. **The apparatuses bolster the counts with straightforward graphical UIs. They** additionally master vide arrange to alter offices with the goal that systems can be effectively changed to

produce multiple "imagine a scenario where" situations. Regularly the apparatuses additionally include a type of adaptation **control to monitor all of these circumstances. Databases for data, for instance, traffic, device, and duty data are** additionally given. In particular, the devices give integration among the different calculations in the suite. The

common calculations for explaining the models can be described as exact fast calculations, accurate moderate calculations, **also, construed counts. Notwithstanding these descriptive strategies, discrete event reenactment is in the like manner normal. Careful brisk counts, for** example, most brief way, least spreading over the tree, and arranging algorithms are

instructed in starting software engineering calculation courses [CORM01]. They can be actualized in all respects just and run proficiently even on exceptionally huge problems. Shockingly, they are delicate as in apparently unimportant modifications to the hidden model can make the calculations improper; the

calculations are not hearty as for model developments. There are various problems for which realized estimations are moderate, here and there very little superior to savage power specification. These are frequently not valuable for commonsense measured issues. The traveling salesman issue (which has noteworthy interchanges applications) is an outstanding case of this sort. For issues without any known gainful calculations, rough just as heuristic techniques can be used. Discrete event diversion, which is a reenactment technique that is acclaimed for exhibiting correspondence structures, is another likelihood. It is the most versatile approach to manage to illustrate. In any case, it tends to be in all respects expensive computationally, especially for huge frameworks. The wide assortment in the trademark times of a correspondence framework makes a united reenactment impracticable. Procedure terms of automated switches and bit times of fiber optic directs are evaluated in nanoseconds, bit times for remote transmission are estimated in microseconds, human response times are in seconds to minutes, and interim between frustrations of specific devices goes upward from months. This makes recreation pursuing all intents and purposes estimated frameworks. Additionally, the size of present-day arranges their high data rates, and the modestly little sizes of ATM cells on other data units makes reproduction restrictively tedious for general use. However, the method is valuable for displaying singular gadgets and complex protocols on little nets. Every single business apparatus that utilization discrete occasion simulation utilizes crossbreed techniques that blend diagnostic and discrete occasion reproduction. The algorithms for entire systems by and large are systematic, while nitty-gritty conduct of switches and different gadgets might be reproduced.

Network Design tools

Net Rule, Analytical Engines, a Java-based instrument for WAN based systems. It has all the earmarks of being exquisite and generally easy to utilize and utilizes primarily scientific algorithms. OPNET Technologies offers a product suite planned to support system specialist organizations. The examination and configuration apparatuses underline integration of expository and reproduction procedures to give exact outcomes in a reasonable time to huge, complex networks.

Network Topology

Topology is the programming of a network. It is the game plan of hubs typically switches, programming switch/switch highlights and associations in a system regularly spoke to as a diagram. The topology of the system and the overall areas of the source and goal of traffic streams on the system decide the ideal way for each stream and the degree to which repetitive choices for steering exist in case of a disappointment. There are two unique methods for portraying framework geometry: the physical topology and the insightful (or sign) topology. The seen topology of a framework is the configuration of hubs and physical associations, including wires (Ethernet, DSL), fiber optics, and microwave. There are a few basic physical topologies, as depicted beneath and as appeared in the delineation.

Sorts of physical topologies

In the transport organize topology, each hub is associated in arrangement directly. This game plan is discovered today fundamentally in link broadband appropriation systems.

In the star arrange topology, a focal hub has an immediate association with every other hub. Exchanged neighborhood (LANs) in light of Ethernet switches, including most wired home and office systems, have a physical star topology.

In the ring system topology, the hubs are associated in a shut circle design. A few rings will pass information just one way, while others are fit for transmission in the two headings. These bidirectional ring systems are stronger than transport systems since traffic can arrive at a hub by moving in either heading. Metro systems dependent on Synchronous Optical Network

Technology (SONET) are the essential case of ring systems today.

The work arranges topology joins hubs with associations so different ways between probably a few points of the system are accessible. A system is said to be completely fit if all hubs are straightforwardly associated with every single other hub and halfway coincided if just a few hubs have various associations with others. Lattice to make various ways builds flexibility under disappointment, yet expands cost. The Internet is a work organize.

The tree arranges topology, additionally called a star of stars, is where star topologies are themselves associated in a star setup. Numerous bigger Ethernet switch systems including server farm systems, are arranged as trees.

Logical topologies

A consistent topology for a system more often than not alludes to the connection among hubs and legitimate associations. A coherent association will vary from a physical way when data can take an undetectable jump at the middle of the road focuses. In optical systems, optical include drop multiplexers (ADMs) make consistent optical ways because the ADM jump isn't unmistakable to the endpoint hubs. Systems dependent on virtual circuits (or passages) will have a physical topology dependent on the genuine association medium (fiber, for instance) and a coherent topology dependent on the circuits/burrows.

Once in awhile the legitimate topology will allude to the topology from the's perspective, which means the availability of the system. IP and Ethernet organize, the two most generally utilized today, are completely coincided at the association level because any client can interface with some other - except if a few methods for blocking undesirable associations, similar to a firewall, is presented. This full availability is a property of the system conventions utilized (IP and Ethernet), not of the system topology itself. Any system topology can seem, by all accounts, to be completely fit its clients.

Ring Topology

This is termed ring configuration because it forms a ring, because each PC is linked with yet a fellow PC, the other one being connected with the first. Just two neighbors for every gadget.

Highlights of Ring Topology Various signal boosters are often used for Ring Topology with such a large amount of hubs provided that somebody needs to send a few information to the last hub in the ring topology with 100 hubs, at that point the information should go through 99 hubs to arrive at the 100th hub. Subsequently to avert information misfortune repeaters are utilized in the system. The transmission is unidirectional, be that as it may, it might be made double directional by having 2 affiliations among each Network Node, it is called double

Ring Topology.

In double Ring Topology, double ring frameworks are confined, and the data stream is a reverse route in them. Likewise, on the off chance that one ring comes up short, the subsequent ring can go about as a reinforcement, to keep the system up. Information is moved in a consecutive way that is a little bit at a time.

Information transmitted needs to go through every hub of the system, till the goal hub.

Pros of Ring Topology

Transmitting system isn't affected by heavy traffic or through along with more core stations, merely because the core stations with coins are capable of transmitting information. Unobstructive to introduce and expand

Cons of Ring Topology

Investigation in ring structure is unpleasant.

Eliminating PCs is pestering the system exercise.

The inability of one PC is irritating to whole structure.

Transport Topology

Transport Topology is a system form where every Computer and system piece of equipment is linked to a lonely link.

If it has two data sources properly, it's termed the Linear Bus Topology.

Characteristics of Bus Topology Information is transmitted in one manner only.

Each device is linked to a unique

Bus Topology Link Strong points.

At the very least, the necessary relation emerged separately with respect to many other context topology.

For use in small organizations It's immediate. Difficult to make to combine two of the junctions.

Shortcomings of Bus Topology

Links the arrows and now the whole structure misses the point. In the event that perhaps the template traffic is friendly or the middle lines are more visible, the structure decreases.

The link has a limited duration. It's lighter than that of the structure of the ring.

Showcases of Star Topology Each core has some kind of connection with an inside point. Concentrate spot is a transmitter for the data flow.

Can be used with distorted pair, Optical Fiber or coaxial connection

Advantages of Star Topology

Quick execution with two or three centers and low framework traffic

Focus can be updated viably.

Easy to examine.

Straightforward to the course of action and alter.

Simply that center is impacted which has failed, rest of the center points can work effectively.

Weaknesses of Star Topology

The Price of the framework is high price to be used in the unlikely event that the emphasis point misses the mark, by then the whole structure is halted because all center points rely on the inside.

Chapter 5: WIDE AREA NETWORK

A wide territory organizes (WAN) is a media communications arrange, normally utilized for associating PCs, which traverses a wide land region, for example, between various urban communities, states, or even nations. WANs normally are utilized by partnerships or associations to encourage the trading of information between their PCs in scattered workplaces. Overall enterprises, most enormous organizations with offices at different areas use WANs, and even free organizations with just two local areas logically use WANs. Most WANs interface at any rate two neighborhood (LANs) and the Internet is on a very basic level an immense WAN.

Even though WANs fill a need like that of LANs, WANs are sorted out and worked out of the blue. The customer of a WAN as a general rule does not have the correspondence lines that interface the remote PC frameworks however rather buys into an administration through a media communications supplier. In contrast to LANs, WANs normally don't connect singular PCs, however rather are used to interface LANs in what are known as internetworks, using devices called switches and remote augmentations. WANs in like manner transmit data at considerably more moderate velocities than LANs, most ordinarily at about 1.5 megabits consistently (Mbps) or less, as opposed to the tens, hundreds, or even a large number of

Mbps achieved by LANs. WANs are fundamentally similar to metropolitan region frameworks (MANs), in any case, are regularly increasingly slow correspondences joins for separations more noteworthy than 50 kilometers.

WANs have existed for quite a long time, yet new advances, administrations, and applications have created throughout the years. WANs were initially created for advanced rented line administrations conveying just voice, instead of information. In that capacity, they associated the private branch exchanges (PBXs) of remote work environments of a comparable association. WANs are up 'til now used for voice organizations, notwithstanding, are used most strongly for data and, as of late, likewise for pictures, for example, video conferencing. WAN usage is creating, as more associations have presented LANs and as continuously moderate internetworking apparatus has ended up being open.

Even though WANs fill a need like that of LANs, WANs are organized and worked unexpectedly. The client of a WAN, for the most part, does not claim the correspondence lines that associate the remote PC frameworks yet rather buys into an administration through a broadcast communications supplier. In contrast to LANs, WANs ordinarily don't interface singular PCs, yet rather are utilized to connect LANs in what are known as internetworks, utilizing gadgets called switches and remote scaffolds. WANs additionally transmit information at much more slow speeds than LANs, most regularly at about 1.5 megabits every second (Mbps) or less, rather than the tens, hundreds, or even a huge number of Mbps accomplished by LANs. WANs are basically like metropolitan zone systems (MANs), yet are ordinarily increasingly slow interchanges joins for separations more noteworthy than 50 kilometers.

WANs have existed for a considerable length of time, yet innovations, administrations, and applications have created throughout the years. WANs were initially created for advanced rented line administrations conveying just voice, instead of information. Accordingly, they associated the private branch trades (PBXs) of remote workplaces of a similar organization. WANs are as yet utilized for voice administrations, however, are utilized most vigorously for information and, as of late, additionally for pictures, for example, video conferencing. WAN utilization is developing, as more organizations have introduced LANs and as progressively moderate internetworking hardware has turned out to be accessible.

Even though WANs fill a need like that of LANs, WANs are sorted out and worked out of the blue. The customer of a WAN normally does not have the correspondence lines that interface the remote PC structures anyway rather gets tied up with an organization through a media interchanges provider. As opposed to LANs, WANs normally don't associate particular

PCs, yet rather are used to interface LANs in what are known as internetworks, using contraptions called switches and remote frameworks. WANs moreover transmit data at significantly more moderate rates than LANs, most for the most part at about 1.5 megabits consistently (Mbps) or less, as opposed to the tens, hundreds, or even a considerable number of Mbps achieved by LANs. WANs are in a general sense like metropolitan zone frameworks (MANs), be that as it may, are conventionally progressively moderate trades joins for partitions more unmistakable than 50 kilometers.

WANs have existed for an extensive timeframe, yet developments, organizations, and applications have made consistently. WANs were at first delivered for cutting edge leased line organizations passing on simply voice, rather than data. Therefore, they related the private branch exchanges (PBXs) of remote work environments of a comparative association. WANs are so far used for voice organizations, nonetheless, are used most seriously for data and, starting late, also for pictures, for instance, video conferencing. WAN use is creating, as more associations have presented LANs and as progressively moderate internetworking equipment has ended up being available.

Point to Point services

The fundamental sort of point-to-point WAN development in North America is TI, which relies upon a strategy for disengaging a propelled line organization with a pace of 1.544 Mbps into 24 channels of 64 Kbps each. By recent rules, this rate is respectably moderate appeared differently concerning LAN advancement and stood out from the extending corporate solicitations set on LANs. The cost of setting up and leasing a TI (or the snappier T3) addresses a sizable expense for associations. In the mid-1990s pretty much all WANs used Ti or other leased lines, which are leased from a media correspondences transporter, yet this changed rapidly as more affordable and faster alternatives rose. Various onlookers have guessed the sharp lessening of leased line benefits once the system is set up to all the more probable assistance the more exceptional, increasingly moderate alternatives. Other point-to-point organizations open consolidate fragmentary Tl, T3, information telephone automated organizations, traded 56 Kbps, composed organizations propelled framework (ISDN), and digressed propelled endorser line (ADSL). ADSL and practically identical DSL developments drew a great deal of thought from corporate framework chairmen in the late 1990s since they were widely more reasonable than leased lines—as much as 60 percent less and passed on relative or better execution.

Despite their average amazing costs, another drawback to point-to-point arrangements is that they aren't fitting to oblige convenient customers, e.g., business voyagers. Since the organizations are associated exceptionally to unequivocal territories, associations must find elective techniques for framework access for versatile customers. Group traded frameworks organization gives this limit, among various points of interest.

Group Switched Services

WAN advancements that rely upon open frameworks utilizing package trading, a system for encoding data into little, amazingly recognized pieces known as groups, have been logically renowned over the earlier decade. Two of the most noteworthy pack based developments are edge hand-off and non concurrent move mode (ATM).

Packaging move is the more prepared of the two, coming into general use in the mid-1990s. It was in the colossal segment a substitution to the slower X.25 standard that had been around since the mid-1970s. Most packaging hand-off WANs are encouraged by business sort out chairmen that charge level rates subject to the speed of organization or volume of data required. Supported by decently modest frameworks organization hardware, diagram handoff relies upon structure up a predictable or virtual circuit over a framework with another PC. In packaging hand-off, the groups, or edges, of data may change in size, and no undertaking is made to address botches. This keeps going part relies upon the assumption that packaging move is continued running over the commonly high gauge, automated frameworks, and the data is less weak to botches. This is like manner improves speed since the framework show isn't endeavoring to address the data. The reliability of this affiliation licenses packaging move master centers to guarantee a particular least level of organization. The close to insignificant exertion and high bore of the organization made edge move one of the most noticeable WAN developments during the 1990s.

ATM organizations, which were introduced monetarily in the mid-1990s, contingent upon relative gauges. Many have touted ATM as a jump forward development, anyway as of the late 1990s it had only an unassuming impact on the WAN market. ATM uses a thought called cell to move to transmit data. Cells are reliably evaluated, little packages of data; by ATM, just 53 bytes each, including a 5-byte header. Then again, a packaging hand-off bundle may range up to a couple of thousand bytes. Correspondingly, similarly as with edge hand-off, ATM moves data over a portrayed virtual path as opposed to empowering groups to seek after any number of approaches to their objectives, as occurs in TCP/IP shows used in Internet applications. This particularly relentless affiliation fits video and various applications that require a reliable, obvious movement of data. The weaknesses to this sureness are that the enduring level of organization may below stood out from various decisions, an ATM may not be all around arranged to regulate transient spikes looked for after for framework resources.

Fiber Optic network

Fiber-optic accessibility for WANs is another huge innovative work in an area. Fiber optics, which incorporates sending light banner through glass or plastic fibers, can reinforce brisk and incredibly astonishing data move. Most fiber-optic frameworks use some sort of group trading advancement, for instance, ATM.

One creating a standard in this field is a synchronous optical framework (SONET), a lot of shows grasped by the American National Standards Institute (ANSI) for high-transmission limit fiber-optic frameworks organization. The all-inclusive easy to SONET is known as the synchronous modernized pecking request (SDH). While its specific advantages have been recognized by a couple of, others note that the monetary issues of SONET are less captivating. It has exhibited expensive to execute, and a couple of critics promise it wasn't organized properly to manage overpowering data traffic that associations need such benefits for. Regardless, gigantic associations with generous throughput necessities have begun to connect to SONET-based organizations.

A battling, and even more fiscally persuading, standard is thick wavelength division multiplexing (DWDM). DWDM is a system for capably sharing give up the fiber by changing the piece of the light go for each phenomenal stream of data. By using each fiber even more capably, DWDM allows inside and out higher exchange speeds for data than SONET, which relies upon time-division multiplexing (TDM) or conveying time to each unique stream of data on a fixed rotate. This proselyte into extensive cost speculation assets on gear as well. DWDM development was overall rapidly sent by different framework overseers because of such focal points. While the Internet and different frameworks organization progressions have changed the quintessence of WANs and have bargained some progressively prepared kinds of WAN development, different authorities acknowledge they will end up being increasingly huge instead of less, as examples can envision globalization and telecommuting make new enthusiasm for high control long-partition arranging. Enthusiasm for framework information move limit will continue swelling. One advancement measure saw corporate WAN traffic climbing by as much as 30 percent a year through 2002, and a lot of this traffic will dynamically be coordinated through open frameworks using virtual private framework development rather than the shut private previous frameworks.

Advantages of WAN

Brings together IT framework-Many think about this present WAN's top preferred position. A WAN takes out the need to purchase email or record servers for every office. Rather, you just need to set up one at your head office's server farm. Setting up a WAN additionally streamlines server the board, since you won't need to help, back-up, host, or physically secure a few units. Additionally, setting up a WAN gives huge economies of scale by giving a focal pool of IT assets the entire organization can take advantage of.

Lifts your security -Setting up a WAN enables you to impart touchy information to every one of your destinations without sending the data over the Internet. Having your WAN scramble your information before you send it includes an additional layer of insurance for any secret material you might move. With such huge numbers of programmers out there simply kicking the bucket to take delicate corporate information, a business needs all the security it can get from system interruptions.

Expands transmission capacity-Corporate WANS regularly utilize rented lines rather than broadband associations with the structure the foundation of their systems. Utilizing rented lines offers a few pluses for an organization, including higher transfer speeds than your run of the mill broadband associations. Corporate WANS additionally commonly offer boundless month to month information move limits, so you can utilize these connections as much as you can imagine without boosting costs. Improved correspondences increment proficiency as well as lift profitability.

Disposes of Need for ISDN-WANs can slash expenses by wiping out the need to lease costly ISDN circuits for telephone calls. Rather, you can have your WAN convey them. If your WAN supplier "organizes voice traffic," you likely won't perceive any drop off in voice quality, either. You may likewise profit by a lot less expensive call rates when contrasted with calls made utilizing ISDN circuits. A few organizations utilize a half and half approach. They have inbound brings come over ISDN and outbound brings go over the WAN. This methodology won't set aside you like a lot of money, yet it will even now bring down your bill.

Ensured uptime-Many WAN suppliers offer business-class support. That implies you get a particular measure of uptime month to month, quarterly, or yearly as a component of your SLA. They may likewise offer you nonstop help. Ensured uptime is a major in addition to regardless of what your industry. Let's be honest. No organization can bear to be down for any time allotment in the present business condition given the stringent requests of current clients.

Cuts costs, increment benefits-notwithstanding taking out the requirement for ISDN, WANs can enable you to cut expenses and increment benefits in a wide assortment of different ways. For instance, WANS kill or altogether decrease the expenses of social occasion groups from various workplaces in a single area. Your promoting group in the United States can work intimately with your assembling group in Germany utilizing video conferencing and email. Saving money on the movement costs alone could make putting resources into a WAN a reasonable alternative for you.

Technical support-Notwithstanding offering help for a wide assortment of utilizations and countless terminals, WANs enable organizations to grow their systems through module associations over areas and lift interconnectivity by utilizing portals, scaffolds, and switches. Besides, by bringing together organize the board and observing of utilization and execution, WANS guarantee the greatest accessibility and unwavering quality.

Disadvantages of WAN

High arrangement costs — WANs are confused and complex, so they are fairly costly to set up. Clearly, the greater the WAN, the costlier it is to set up. One reason that the arrangement expenses are high is the need to associate remote zones. In any case, by utilizing open systems, you can set up a WAN utilizing just programming (SD-WAN), which diminishes arrangement costs. Remember additionally that the value/execution proportion of WANs is preferable now over 10 years or so back.

Security Concerns — WANs open the path for particular sorts of inward security breaks, for example, unapproved use, data robbery, and malignant harm to documents. While numerous organizations have some security set up with regards to the branches, they send the majority of their security at their server farms to control and oversee data sent to their areas. This technique decreases the executives' costs yet restrains the organization's capacity to manage security breaks at their areas. A few organizations additionally experience serious difficulties compacting and quickening SSL traffic without fundamentally expanding security vulnerabilities and making new administration challenges.

Support Issues-Maintaining a WAN is a test, no uncertainty about it. Ensuring that your server farm will be up and working every minute of every day is the greatest upkeep challenge of all. Server farm supervisors must most likely distinguish disappointments before they happen and decrease server farm personal time however much as could reasonably be expected, paying little respect to the reasons.

Chapter 6: Configuration

Windows servers

The accomplishment of an established development undertaking depends upon wary orchestrating got together with cautious execution. You need to start by portraying the degree of the errand with the objective you know where you're going to have to spin up. By then, you just have to develop an effort plan that includes prototype testing to adjust to the new organization and to see any future problems which may occur during most of the motion technique. In addition, a thorough assessment of your current situation is crucial to guarantee that no curve balls come in. A technique should be used to relocate current computers and professions. Eventually, once development is in progress, continuous experimentation should be carried out to guarantee that all is done as a mastermind.

Migration situations

Relocation errands including servers can be requested in different ways, dependent upon whether you are passing on another structure, refreshing or joining a present framework, or executing another establishment model, for instance, dispersed processing. In addition, advances may vary based on whether you move your entire premise or just part of it; paying little attention to whether you intend to reuse current equipment or move to fresh hardware; whether your situation is monitored or uncontrolled; regardless your current structure is large or small, bound together or encircled, heterogeneous or homogeneous; and whether it is different. With the such tremendous quantities of different strategies for envisioning and checking establishment migration stretches out, there is no single method to manage how such exercises should be masterminded and executed. In any case, there are a couple of stages and examinations that are ordinary to all relocation broadens, and observing such endorsed systems and completing They can assist guarantee the success of the excursion. I will start by describing the six necessary migration conditions for affiliates who need to overuse the latest characteristics and capabilities discovered in Windows Server 2012.

Greenfield

So far as the institution is concerned, a greenfield scheme is such that there is currently no building at all. Presume, for instance, that company X Is yet another organization beginning up which requires an on-site institution sent to work quickly. Greenfield carries on a framework that is dependent on Windows Server 2012 will join developments such as: constructing, gathering and understanding the vital context for setting up contacts, segments and distinct organizational processes. Buying the framework equipment which has been secured for Windows Server 2012.

Performing a prototype allows you to choose if the orchestrated framework will satisfy your company requirements and to guess any future problems that may arise during the carry-out. Showing your education scheme using any strategy tools you've been using. The normal favourite position of a startup motion is that it gives you the chance to get what needed to be done right from the beginning. Organizations are constantly making strides and are stationary, so giving little attention to how you are carefully considering future enhancement, you can, however, be confronted with difficulties in propelling your institution to deal with occurrences such as partnerships, purchases and sub-venture claims to reputation divisions. In conjunction, as a dose of reality, almost all of the customers of this quick start guide who are intending to update their capacity for intervention are likely to enter into company with organizations that have, in any case, one of the current Active Directory trees established and are talking about shifting them to Windows Server 2012, which is the associated implementation situation.

Boondocks update

Managers of Active Directory circumstances have by and large Be wary, or even shaky, of conducting maps updates using Adprep.exe order line utility. Introduction of each different type of Windows Server, a further instance design arises in the same way, but before that, the attempt to introduce land controllers operating a type of Windows Server for your current Active Directory has taken that you also set up your Active Directory by upgrading the system. The willingness of managers to make such changes relies, metaphorically speaking, on three issues: the method of upgrading a woodland instance using Adprep was most of the moment a stumbling block on previous variants Windows Host includes the use of a broad range of certifications to log onto unmistakable space servers, copy Adprep documents, and operate Adprep from the request line with different parameters. The more incredible the approach, the further recognizable the description of the botch is.

There is a likelihood that anything was going on may turn out severely during the mapping overhaul process, achieving degenerate timberland that anticipates that you should play out a woodlands recovery, which can be an irksome and repetitive methodology.

There was the probability that the arrangement redesign may go off well yet realize indications, for instance, adventure applications that break and never again work suitably. The endorsed approach to manage to keep up a vital good ways from such issues is to make a test circumstance that mirrors your creation condition the extent that its Active Directory design, arrange organizations, and business applications. By upgrading the organization of your test boondocks using Adprep, you would then have the option to all the more probable imagine any issues that may arise when you update the development of your age timberland

Mixed condition

As you found in the past development circumstance, existing associations that need to abuse the new limits of Windows Server 2012 can do thusly without removing their system and superseding it with another. They should just Implement computers running on Windows Server 2012 to their status and progress them as room processors. Doing it now usually recharges the recipe, and management can increase the woods and room minimalist standard to Windows Server 2012 with little fear of adversely affecting their current apps and organization. Having to pay little character to that one, however, ensure you last test your growth update and useful adjustments in the test situation that reflects your birth situation just to ensure that there will be no problems that can affect your company. In either case, many features of Windows Server 2012 can be performed in the same way as existing content taking off basic upgrades to the present boondocks, for instance, overhauling the mapping or raising the forest or space valuable levels.

Essential steps of configuring a new server

Client Configuration

The absolute first thing you're going to need to do, on the off chance that it wasn't a piece of your OS arrangement, is to change the root secret word. This ought to act naturally obvious, yet can be shockingly disregarded during a standard server arrangement. The secret word ought to be in any event 8 characters, utilizing a mix of upper and lowercase letters, numbers and images. You should likewise set up a secret word strategy that indicates maturing, locking, history and unpredictability necessities on the off chance that you are going to utilize neighborhood accounts. By and large, you should cripple the root client totally and make non-favored client accounts with sudo access for the individuals who require raised rights.

System Configuration

One of the most fundamental designs you'll have to make is to empower arrange network by doling out the server an IP address and hostname. For most servers, you'll need to utilize a static IP so customers can generally discover the asset at a similar location. On the off chance that your system utilizes

VLANs, think about how disengaged the server's portion is and where it would best fit. On the off chance that you don't utilize IPv6, turn it off. Set the hostname, area and DNS server data. At least two DNS servers ought to be utilized for repetition and you should test and look up to ensure name goals is working effectively.

Bundle Management

You're setting up your new server for a particular reason, so ensure you introduce whatever bundles you may require if they aren't a piece of the dispersion you're utilizing. These could be application bundles like PHP, MongoDB, Nginx or supporting bundles like the pear. Similarly, any incidental bundles that are introduced on your framework ought to be expelled to recoil the server impression. The majority of this ought to be done through your conveyance's bundle the executives' arrangement, for example, yum or adept for simpler administration not far off.

Update Installation and Configuration

When you have the correct bundles introduced on your server, you should ensure everything is refreshed. The bundles you introduced, yet the piece and default bundles too. Except if you have a necessity for a particular variant, you ought to consistently utilize the most recent creation discharge to keep your framework secure. More often than not, your bundle the board arrangement will convey the most up to date upheld rendition. You ought to likewise consider setting up programmed refreshes inside the bundle the executives device if doing as such works for the service(s) you're facilitating on this server.

NTP Configuration

Arrange your server to match up to its opportunity to NTP servers. These could be inside NTP servers if your condition has those, or outside time servers that are accessible for anybody. What's significant is to avoid clock float, where the server's clock slants from the genuine time. This can cause a lot of issues, including confirmation issues where time slant between the server and the validating framework is estimated before allowing access. This ought to be a straightforward change, yet it's a basic piece of a solid foundation.

Firewalls and iptables

Contingent upon your circulation, iptables may as of now be secured and expect you to open what you need, yet paying little mind to the default configuration, you ought to consistently investigate it and ensure it's set up how you need. Make sure to consistently utilize the guideline of least benefit and just open those ports you completely required for the administrations on that server. If your server is behind a committed firewall or some likeness thereof, make certain to deny everything except for what's vital there too. Accepting your firewall IS prohibitive as a matter of course; remember to open up what you require for your server to carry out its responsibility.

Verifying SSH

SSH is the fundamental remote access strategy for Linux circulations and all things considered ought to be appropriately verified. You should cripple root's capacity to SSH in remotely, regardless of whether you handicapped the record with the goal that just if there should arise an occurrence of root gets empowered on the server for reasons unknown despite everything it won't be exploitable remotely. You can likewise confine SSH to certain IP ranges on the off chance that you have a fixed arrangement of customer IPs that will interface. Alternatively, you can change the default SSH port to "darken" it, yet truly, a basic sweep will uncover the new open port to any individual who needs to discover it. At long last, you can impair secret key validation through and through and use declaration based confirmation to lessen considerably further the odds of SSH abuse.

Daemon Configuration

You've tidied up your bundles, but at the same time, it's critical to set the correct applications to auto-start on reboot. Make certain to mood killer any daemons you needn't bother with.

One key to a safe server is lessening the dynamic impression however much as could be expected so the main surface territories accessible for the assault are those required by the application(s). When this is done, outstanding administrations ought to be solidified however much as could be expected to guarantee versatility.

SELinux and Further Hardening

On the off chance that you've at any point utilized a Red Hat distro, you may be comfortable with SELinux, the portion solidifying apparatus that shields the framework from different activities. SELinux is extraordinary at ensuring against unapproved use and access to framework assets. It's likewise extraordinary at breaking applications, so ensure you test your setup out with SELinux empowered and utilize the logs to ensure nothing real is being blocked.

Logging

At long last, you should ensure that the degree of logging you need is empowered and that you have adequate assets for it. You will wind up investigating this server, so help yourself out now and manufacture the logging structure you'll have to tackle issues rapidly. Most programming has configurable logging, however, you'll require some experimentation to locate the correct harmony between insufficient data and to an extreme. There are a large group of outsider logging instruments that can help including collection to perception, yet every condition should be considered for its needs first. At that point, you can discover the tool(s) that will enable you to fill them.

Every single one of these means can set aside some effort to actualize, particularly the first run through around. Be that as it may, by setting up a daily schedule of beginning server design, you can guarantee that new machines in your condition will be versatile. Inability to make any of these strides can prompt truly genuine results if your server is ever the objective of an assault. Tailing them won't ensure wellbeing - information breaks occur however it makes it undeniably progressively hard for pernicious on-screen characters and will require some level of ability to survive.

Advantages of having servers

A server offers you a mess of dependability. A server, then again, is a powerful answer for such a significant issue. Server equipment keeps up excess equipment to handle these issues at minute's notice.

In such cases, the disappointment of one gadget doesn't ensure the disappointment of the whole server framework. In this way, it can keep on serving your business with full zeal even after the disappointment of an unimportant little related gadget, in contrast to your interlinked PCs. Dependability you needed, the unwavering quality you'll get.

A server furnishes your business with system security

This can be viewed as truly outstanding and most critical advantages of a server. By making the recognized gathering and individual records, an individual right can be relegated to clients dependent on the nature and measure of information they can access based on their necessities. This can cut down unapproved information access, all things considered and can give your system extra security that you had hungered for previously. On the off chance that you have a business group and an HR group in your organization, both would not have the option to get to the information of each other regardless of whether the whole information is available on a solitary server.

A server gives your business a consistent remote openness

A Windows 2008 server would give you the alternative to have 2 remote clients on its system simultaneously of course. What's more, it likewise offers you the chance to include the same number of remote clients you need sooner rather than later through Remote Desktop allowance. Hence, land boundaries stop to be an issue any longer. Your laborers will most likely work remotely and access records on your server at whatever point they need any place they are. They would likewise have the option to get to their organization messages from any internet browser on their particular gadgets at whatever point they need from anyplace on the planet.

A server furnishes your business with a brought together reinforcement office

Information misfortunes happen generally in working environments for a few reasons running from machine disappointments to indiscretion. These things make tremendous issues particularly when the work environment works without a server. A server can be viewed as a gift in this angle since it helps a great deal in smoothing up your information reinforcement process. You will almost certainly back up the entirety of your information including your messages to unified capacity on your server and lessen every one of the problems related with information misfortunes subsequently, improving your work environment efficiency simultaneously.

A server framework helps in legitimate infection the board

Perhaps the best danger looked by your system is a conceivable infection or spyware disease. Consequently, an antivirus framework is an outright need nowadays. A server framework can help a ton in advantageous infection the executives. The framework director will almost certainly send the counter infection programming from a solitary PC to every workstation PC associated on the system, run a system-wide filter in general (counting the gadgets associated on the WiFi system) and evacuate a wide range of infections assuming any. So you can see that this accommodation is fundamentally unrivaled. Because of the minimized server framework, the whole infection the executives' procedure should be possible from a solitary PC itself. Continuously recollect that costs caused in making a server-based system aren't only an expense. It's speculation; a contribute having high ROI particularly when your independent company adventure is concerned. It's certainly going to profit you over the long haul.

Disadvantages' of having a server

1. High Costs

The most evident point about having a Server-based system is the expanded expense. Servers are substantially more costly than PC's to gain and you should become accustomed to expanded costs for Server-based programming as well.

Servers don't keep going forever and are commonly repetitive following 5 years for everything except the most essential of capacities. Windows and Mac Servers are authorized 'per client' so as you increment the quantity of staff, these organizations will need their offer as well! Servers do require ordinary checking, refreshing, and observing. All things considered, you should attempt changes in clients, consents, email locations and this may require some itemized IT information. Also, if Servers turn out badly, they will be in all respects expensive to fix. While producers regularly offer sensibly estimated equipment guarantees, they will wash their hands of any issue with the Software (regardless of whether brought about by the equipment issue) and as specially appointed IT to bolster will rapidly include, numerous associations structure some sort of agreement with their Server providers/installers. This bodes well as the organization that introduced your framework ought to be in a decent position to have the option to look after it. Hope to pay a noteworthy sum may be significantly more than you paid for the establishment - for a complete help contract.

2. *Single-purpose of disappointment*

In concentrating your documents and programming in the way portrayed above, you can't abstain from making a solitary purpose of disappointment in your system. If somebody takes or loses the way to your sparkling new

'focal file organizer' your work will endure colossally. While a critical level of the expense of procuring a Server goes towards enhancing the dangers of disappointment, the probability of noteworthy 'down-time' is consistently there. A consistently observed reinforcement framework, RAID cluster, and an uninterruptible power supply (UPS) ought to be considered as an absolute minimum, however and, after it's all said and done blackouts of different sorts can and do occur.

3. *Progress*

The procedure of progress from a non-server system to a Server-based one can be inconvenient what's more, is sure to include disturbance to PC clients just as changes in the manner they work. This is particularly the situation with a Windows-based Server, as the connection among PC's and Servers in a Windows domain rotates around a client account which will be not quite the same as the one you at present use. At the very least, this involves moving work area settings just like records, top picks and perhaps email to the new account and may even include reinstalling or reconfiguring printers, antivirus programming, and different projects as well. When getting ready for another Server at that point, it is imperative to separate the highlights and programming you should have in this new condition. The disturbance caused to your staff and different clients is best limited by keeping them educated on how things may change. This can be a significant tedious and needs somebody inside your association with some IT learning to deal with it effectively.

4. *Nature of help*

Disengaging the reason for a given issue is one of the most troublesome parts of ICT support. When an individual from staff can't get an email for instance, would they say they are accomplishing something incorrectly? Is there a major issue with their PC? Is there a system issue? Is it an issue with the

Server? Maybe the ISP is to blame? Or then again even the facilitating organization? Adding a Server to your system includes layers of multifaceted nature and is sure to befuddle these issues. It is essential then that you approach great quality, far-reaching and educated ICT support. The provider ought to be equipped for diagnosing and settling issues at any of these levels to stay away from the bad dream of 'buck-going' between various organizations. Such help can be costly and laden with hazy areas where duty is vague. Ensure you read the agreement!

Conclusion

Thank you for making it through to the end of the Computer Networking course. I hope that it was informative and able to provide you with all the basic tools you need to achieve your goals.

The next step is to take note of what you read and put it into practice. In this case, you will now be able to explain and tell what needs you may be required in terms of networking. You are now able to explain the terms and also knowledgeable about how things work. Some of the things that you have learned include the Wireless networks, system models and also Addresses and IPs. You have further learned on the internet, including the history of the internet, and also the pros and cons that it has brought about in the world.

Did you know the details on storage architecture? Well, now you know more on these and also network-attached storage, storage area network, as well as, tape and tape libraries. Further, you have been enlightened about data patterns and virtualization architecture. This book has given you great and detailed content on TCP and implementation. This include's, layers of TCP, the benefits and also details on the Round Trip Time.

The author has taken you through the details of planning a network. In these, you have gotten the skills on; Organization set up, strategy and culture, options analysis as well as implementation. Network topology has been broken down as well as the design tools.

I believe that this book has enlightened you on the WAN. This includes the point to point services, bundle switched services, the fiber connectivity, and you have also learned the advantages and disadvantages of WAN.

Finally, the author has discussed on the configuration windows server. You have learned step by step the essential steps of configuring a new server.

Finally, if you found this book useful in any way, a review on Amazon is always appreciated!

www.ingramcontent.com/pod-product-compliance
Lightning Source LLC
LaVergne TN
LVHW051242050326
832903LV00028B/2521